CAMDEN MARKET 6

Workbook mit Lösungen

Erarbeitet von
Sigrid Boinski und Petra Günther

unter Mitwirkung der Redaktion
Julia Mohm

**Herausgeber der bisherigen Reihe
und Berater der Programmleitung**
Otfried Börner, StD a.D.,
Dr. phil. h.c. Christoph Edelhoff, StD a.D.,

Fachliche Beratung
Bianka Gehler, Julia Grossmann, Kathrin Hough,
Holger Nürnberg, Alexander Schülting
und Gisela Vogt

Diesterweg
westermann

Symbole

  Dieser Text ist auf der CD für Lehrer und auf der CD für Schüler.

 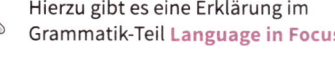 Das Video befindet sich auf der DVD für Lehrer.

 Hierzu gibt es eine Erklärung im Grammatik-Teil Language in Focus.

 Dieses Symbol zeigt die passende Übung im Textbook an.

Die Techniken auf den How to ...-Seiten im Textbook helfen beim Englischlernen.

In den Wordbanks im Textbook befinden sich die wichtigsten Wörter zu einem Thema.

 Der Mond kennzeichnet einfachere Parallelaufgaben zu Aufgaben im Basis-Teil des Textbooks.

 Die Sonne kennzeichnet schwierigere Parallelaufgaben zu Aufgaben im More-Teil des Textbooks.

 Kompetenz: Sprechen

 Kompetenz: Leseverstehen

 Kompetenz: Schreiben

 Kompetenz: Hörverstehen

 Kompetenz: Hörsehverstehen

 Kompetenz: Sprachmittlung

1 Growing up

a) **Think about what could happen in the next few years. Look at the box for ideas.**

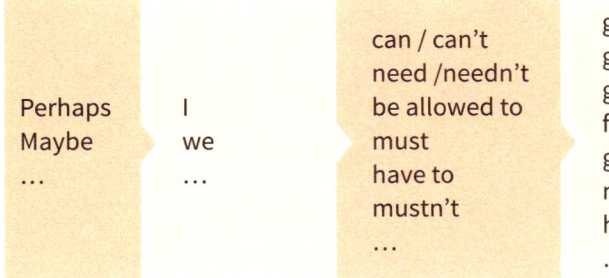

| Perhaps Maybe … | I we … | can / can't need /needn't be allowed to must have to mustn't … | get a job I really want. go to school. go to university. follow a lot of rules. go to another country. move away. have to work. … |

b) **Talk to a partner about what you think could happen.**

Perhaps I have to move away.

Maybe I can go to university.

2 Joan Lingard ⇨ L p. 125

Joan Lingard is the author of the book 'Across the barricades'.
Write a text about Joan Lingard for your school magazine. Look at the boxes for help.

British writer – born in Edinburgh 1932

grew up Belfast – lived until 18

started to write – eleven years old

married, husband Martin

1970 first children's book – "The Twelfth Day of July"

beginning of series of books

Catholic Kevin and Protestant Sadie – caught up in troubles in Northern Ireland

_____

_____

_____

_____

_____

_____

_____

_____

3 Feelings

a) Read the words below and sort them into the grid.

positive	negative
optimistic	upset
wonderful	bored
peaceful	helpless
excited	tired
glad	disappointed
free	awful
comfortable	

upset   excited
optimistic   glad
wonderful   tired
peaceful   disappointed
bored   awful
helpless   free
comfortable

b) Read the texts on page 18 and 19 of your textbook again.
Then find the right words for these situations. You can write down more than one word.   ⇨ L p. 125

1. How does Sadie feel when she hears her mother's tirade?

_____

2. How do Sadie's parents feel when she says 'I can go if I want to'?

_____

3. How does Kevin feel about Brian Rafferty's questions?

_____

4 Talking about the book

L 2.11 S 15

a) Listen to Paula. What does she think about 'Across the barricades'?   ⇨ L p. 125

_____

_____

b) Listen again. Then answer the questions.

1 When was the book published?

     1982

     2002

     ✔ 1972

2 What was the first book in the Kevin and Sadie series called?

     The twelfth of June.

     ✔ The twelfth of July.

     The twelfth of May.

3 Why did Paula like the book?

     She thought it was funny.

     ✔ She thought it was interesting and moving.

     She thought it was romantic.

4 How many books about Kevin and Sadie are there?

     three

     four

     ✔ five

5 What's next?

 Do exercises 4a) on page 19 in your textbook

b) 🌙 If you were Sadie's best friend, what advice would you give her? Tick (✓) the things you would say.

I think you should
stop seeing Kevin.

Go away with Kevin.

Your parents should
meet Kevin.

Never talk to Kevin again.

Maybe you should
move to another city.

If you love Kevin you
should be with him.

6 The Troubles

⇨ L p. 125

a) Look at the pictures. What can you see? What do you find interesting, shocking or surprising?
What do you think happened?

b) Read the article about the conflict in Northern Ireland. Then answer the questions. ⇨ L p. 125

The Troubles is the name given to a violent thirty-year period of conflict in Northern Ireland at the end of the 20th century. The conflict began in the late 1960s and it lasted until 1998. Although the Troubles mainly took place in Northern Ireland, some attacks also happened in the Republic of Ireland, England and Europe.

The main issue was the constitutional status of Northern Ireland. Unionists/loyalists, who are mostly Protestants wanted Northern Ireland to remain within the United Kingdom. Irish nationalists/republicans, who are mostly Catholics, wanted Northern Ireland to leave the United Kingdom and join a united Ireland. The conflict began during a campaign to end discrimination against the Catholic/nationalist minority. Loyalists were against the campaign and reacted with violence. British troops were then sent to Northern Ireland.

More than 3,500 people were killed during the Troubles. The worst years of the conflict were 1970 to 1972. In 1972 nearly 500 people were killed.

There was a temporary ceasefire in 1972. The involved parties and the British government held talks to try and end the conflict. They couldn't agree though and the UK government in London pushed through an emergency law which meant that Northern Ireland was under "direct rule" from London. Before that Northern Ireland had its own parliament, the Stormont. Direct rule was only supposed to be for a short while but the unionists and nationalists couldn't agree on how to run Northern Ireland. The Troubles continued throughout the 1970s, 1980s and 1990s. There were "no-go areas" in Belfast and Derry where even the British army couldn't enter. Eventually a process of negotiations began in the late 1990s. This led to the Good Friday Agreement of 1998. One part of the Agreement is that Northern Ireland will remain within the United Kingdom unless a majority of the Northern Irish electorate vote otherwise. It also established the Northern Ireland Executive, a power-sharing government, which must consist of both unionist and nationalist parties.

1 What was the conflict mainly about?

_____

2 How long did the conflict last?

_____

3 How did it end?

_____

7 Leaving 👓

 Do exercise 6 a) on page 20 in your textbook.

b) 🌙 How does Kevin feel? Tick (✓) what you think.

1 ✓ Kevin is in love with Sadie.

☐ Kevin wants to break up with Sadie.

2 ✓ Kevin wants to leave Belfast.

☐ Kevin wants to stay in Belfast.

3 ☐ Kevin thinks the fighting is good.

✓ Kevin hates the fighting.

4 ☐ Kevin is happy with his life.

✓ Kevin wants a better life.

5 ✓ Kevin thinks that life in Northern Ireland is good.

☐ Kevin hates his life in Northern Ireland.

6 ☐ Kevin asks Sadie to come with him.

✓ Kevin doesn't ask Sadie to come with him.

8 At the harbour 🔍

Write down what happened at the harbour. Use the correct tenses.

1 After Kevin (arrive) at the harbour, he (see) Sadie and (run) towards her.

After Kevin had arrived at the harbour, he saw Sadie and ran towards her.

2 After she (tell) him that she was coming to England with him, he (lift) her up and (whirl) her around.

After she had told him that she was coming to England with him, he lifted her up and whirled her around.

3 Before Sadie (go) to the harbour to meet Kevin, she (buy) a ticket for the trip to Liverpool.

Before Sadie went to the harbour to meet Kevin, she had bought a ticket for the trip to Liverpool.

4 Because she (leave) home in secret, Sadie (not have) any luggage.

Because she had left home in secret, Sadie didn't have any luggage.

5 After they (decide) to leave Ireland together, Kevin (take) Sadie's hand and they (walk) to the white, waiting ship.

After they had decided to leave Ireland together, Kevin took Sadie's hand and they walked to the white, waiting ship.

9 Goodbye ✏️

⇨ L p. 125

Imagine you are Sadie or Kevin. Write a letter to your parents explaining why you are leaving.

_____

_____

_____

_____

_____

_____

_____

_____

_____

_____

_____

10 Buddy Holly: Dearest

a) Read the lyrics of the song. Highlight all adjectives in yellow and all verbs in green.

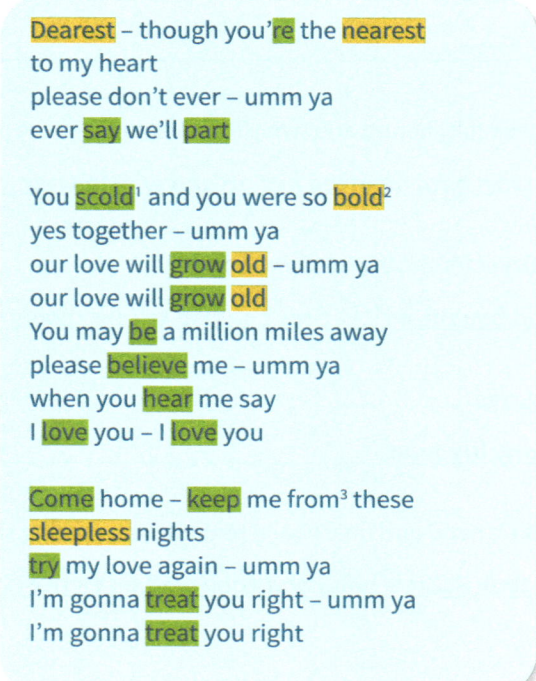

Dearest – though you're the nearest
to my heart
please don't ever – umm ya
ever say we'll part

You scold[1] and you were so bold[2]
yes together – umm ya
our love will grow old – umm ya
our love will grow old
You may be a million miles away
please believe me – umm ya
when you hear me say
I love you – I love you

Come home – keep me from[3] these
sleepless nights
try my love again – umm ya
I'm gonna treat you right – umm ya
I'm gonna treat you right

[1]scold – ausschimpfen; [2]bold – frech, dreist, kühn;
[3]to keep so. from sth – jemand vor etw. bewahren

b) Find the English verbs for:

sich trennen ___*part*___   alt werden ___*grow old*___

behandeln ___*treat*___   versuchen ___*try*___

glauben ___*believe*___

c) Look at some adjectives from the song and write them down like this:

bold – bolder – boldest • frech; dreist

dear – dearer – dearest • lieb

old – older – oldest • alt

near – nearer – nearest • nah

d) Which word in the song text is used as a noun and as a verb?

love

11 Talking about Juno 🇬🇧

Cindy has just watched the film 'Juno'. She wants to tell her sister's English friend Alex what it is about but Cindy only speaks German and Alex only speaks English. Can you help them? Complete the sentences.

Cindy: Es geht um Juno McGuff. Sie ist 16 und wird ungewollt schwanger.

You: Cindy said the film is about __a girl called Juno McGuff. She's 16 and gets pregnant__

__by accident.__

Alex: Well this is really nothing new and happens every day.

You: Alex sagt, __dass dies nichts Ungewöhnliches ist und jeden Tag passiert.__

Cindy: Juno ist etwas Besonderes. Sie macht sich viele Gedanken über ihr Baby.

You: OK, Juno is very special __because she thinks a lot about her baby.__

Alex: OK, I see. And what about her parents?

You: Er fragt __was ihre Eltern dazu meinen.__

Cindy: Sie sind zuerst schockiert, aber dann helfen sie ihr und unterstützen sie.

You: At first they __are shocked, but then they help and support her.__

Alex: Well, now I have an idea what makes the film so special. Thanks!

12 What to do 🔍

Look at some more statements from the film.
Put them into reported speech. Be careful with the tenses.

1 Juno: "I'm really sorry I had sex with you."

Juno told Paulie __that she was really sorry she had had sex with him.__

2 Juno's parents: "Have you thought about having an abortion?"

Juno's parents wanted to know __if Juno had thought about having an abortion.__

3 Juno: "I have found the perfect couple for the baby."

Juno said __that she had found the perfect couple for the baby.__

4 Paulie: "I think you're beautiful."

Paulie told Juno __that he thought she was beautiful.__

5 Doctor: "Do you want to know whether it's a boy or a girl?"

The doctor asked Juno __if she wanted to know whether it was a boy or a girl.__

13 Am I the father?

L 2.12 S 16

a) Shane's girlfriend has just told him that she is pregnant. Listen to his call to the American Pregnancy Helpline. How did his girlfriend tell him about the pregnancy?

She sent him a text message.

b) Listen again and tick (✓) the correct statements.

1 ✓ Shane is 17.

   ☐ Shane is 15.

   ☐ Shane is 20.

   ☐ Shane is 14.

2 ☐ Shane and his girlfriend have been together for three years.

   ☐ Shane and his girlfriend have wanted a baby for a long time.

   ☐ Shane and his girlfriend are no longer a couple.

   ✓ Shane and his girlfriend have been together for three months.

3 ☐ Shane wants his girlfriend to have an abortion.

   ☐ Shane's girlfriend doesn't know yet what she wants to do.

   ☐ Shane wants to keep the baby.

   ✓ Shane's girlfriend wants to bring up the baby herself.

4 ☐ Shane's girlfriend doesn't want him to do a DNA test.

   ☐ Shane thinks he is the father.

   ✓ Shane isn't sure that he is the father.

   ☐ Shane's girlfriend doesn't think he is the father.

5 ✓ Shane has a lot of questions.

   ☐ Shane's girlfriend has a lot of questions.

   ☐ Shane doesn't want to ask anything.

   ☐ Shane hasn't got any questions.

6 ✓ If Shane is the father, he will have certain rights.

   ☐ If Shane is the father, he won't have any rights.

   ☐ If Shane is the father, he can decide the name of the child.

   ☐ If Shane is the father, he will have to live with the mother.

7 ✓ Shane and his girlfriend can get counselling for free.

   ☐ Shane and his girlfriend should talk to their teachers.

   ☐ Shane and his girlfriend should talk to their friends.

   ☐ Shane and his girlfriend shouldn't talk to anyone.

Auf den Test-yourself-Seiten hast du Gelegenheit zu überprüfen, was du in Theme 1 gelernt hast. Bearbeite erst einmal der Reihe nach alle Aufgaben. Überlege anschließend, welche Aufgaben dir leicht gefallen sind, welche nicht ganz einfach waren und welche du richtig schwierig fandest. Deine Ergebnisse kannst du mit den Lösungen hinten im Workbook vergleichen und dann deine Punktzahl eintragen. Dort findest du auch Lerntipps für die Vorbereitung der nächsten Klassenarbeit. Die Test-yourself-Seiten helfen dir bei deiner Selbsteinschätzung mit den Portfolio-Fragebögen.

1 Listening: Needing help ⇨ **L p. 109**  **L 2.13 S 17**

a) Listen to the phone call. Why does the girl call the helpline?

_____

b) Listen again. Then tick (✓) the right answer.

1 The girl hasn't taken a pregnancy test because ...

    she doesn't want to know.

    she's sure she's pregnant.

    she is worried someone will find out.

    she's sure she isn't pregnant.

2 The girl ...

    has got to go to a doctor to get a pregnancy test.

    can buy a home pregnancy test anywhere.

    needs her mum to buy the test.

    has to do the test at school.

3 The woman tells the girl, that ...

    she will have a lot of options if she's pregnant.

    she will have to give the child up for adoption.

    she will have to get married.

    she can bring up the child alone.

4 The girls wants to ...

    take the test with her boyfriend.

    take the test with her mum.

    take the test with her best friend.

    take the test with her teacher.

von **10**

2 Writing: YOUR plan ⇨ **L p. 109**

Write about your life in ten years. Think about:
- what job you will have
- if you will live with a partner
- if you'll have children
- who will do the household duties in your home
- ...

_____

_____

_____

_____

_____

_____

_____

_____

von **15**

3 Reading: Home life 👓

⇨ L p. 109

Read what the people say. Then tick (✓) if the statements are true, false or not in the text.

Greg (23): I've just moved in with my girlfriend. She makes me do a lot of stuff at home. When I was living with my parents my mum did everything. She did the shopping, cooking, cleaning and so on. That was an easy
5 life for me. My girlfriend wants us to split everything. One week I have to do everything and the next week she does it. It's ok though. I actually think it's fairer this way.

Heather (32): I live with my girlfriend and our two
10 children in a 3 bedroom flat. It's important to keep everything tidy and clean, because the flat is so small. My girlfriend doesn't like to do things at home so I normally do the cleaning and washing and she does the shopping. Shopping is a lot less work but it's ok. I like cleaning.

Jack (48): My wife works a lot. She's a nurse and she 15 often has to work at night and at the weekends. I have a part time job, I only work 3 days a week. So I normally do most of the things at home; cleaning, tidying and so on. I also go shopping and I normally do the cooking. When my wife is at home she likes to cook though. 20 She's a much better cook than me anyway.

James (19): I live with three other boys. We share a nice flat but we're all super lazy. The flat looks dreadful. It's always dirty and there's always stuff lying around. My 25 flatmates are nice but I wish they would do more at home. I miss my parents' clean and tidy house. I don't want to do everything though but at least I keep my room clean.

	true	false	not in the text	evidence
				line:
1 Greg's girlfriend does everything at home.				
2 Greg misses living with his mum.				
3 Heather wants to keep the flat tidy and clean.				
4 Heather's girlfriend does the shopping.				
5 Jack often works at night.				
6 Jack does most of the things at home.				
7 James misses his parents' house.				
8 James' room is very small.				

von **16**

4 Grammar: About 'Juno' 🔍

⇨ L p. 109

What did the people say about Juno? Read the sentences and put them into reported speech.

Mariah: "This is the best film I have ever seen."

_____

Rick: "Ellen Page is a talented actress."

_____

Cynthia: "I liked the songs best."

_____

Nathalie: "The parents in the film are really helpful and understanding."

_____

von **5**

Brad: "Young people who watch the film will think more about teenage pregnancy."

_____

E1 Listening: Juno on the screen

a) Listen to five people being interviewed. Who says what? Write the correct letters in the boxes:
(R = Rob, J = Jessica, M = Mike, E = Emma, S = Sarah)

 L 1.5 S 1

J	The dialogue just didn't sound natural.	M	Overall I really liked it.
R	I laughed all the way through the film.	S	I thought that a lot of it was unrealistic.
M	I was able to relate to the characters.	E	I especially like the strong feminist character Juno.
S	Teenage pregnancy isn't really like that at all.	J	I didn't think that the jokes were very funny.
E	I think Ellen Page is a great actress.	R	It left you with that warm feeling inside.

> **How to …**
> listen
> TB p.174

b) Now sort the statements from a) into the table below.

positive (+)	negative (-)
I laughed all the way through the film.	*The dialogue just didn't sound natural.*
I was able to relate to the characters.	*Teenage pregnancy isn't really like that at all.*
I think Ellen Page is a great actress.	*I thought that a lot of it was unrealistic.*
Overall I really liked it.	*I didn't think that the jokes were very funny.*
I especially like the strong feminist character Juno.	
It left you with that warm feeling inside.	

E2 Writing: About Kevin ⇨ L p. 125

Write a short text about Kevin. Look at the info for help.

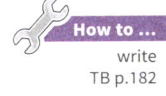

18 years old

Catholic

eight brothers and sisters

unskilled worker

Belfast, Northern Ireland

wants to move to London

Kevin McCoy

girlfriend: Sadie

> **How to …**
> write
> TB p.182

_____

_____

_____

_____

_____

_____

_____

_____

_____

E3 Reading: A good solution 👓

Read Austin's story. Then tick (✓) if the statements are right or wrong. Write down where you found the information.

How to ...
read
TB p.174

> I met Kaylee at the beginning of sophomore year in high school. We were both 15 and we fell madly in love. I had never had a girlfriend before and it was Kaylee's first relationship too. We went to the mall after school, watched movies or went to the diner to have burgers and milkshakes. It was great. Kaylee and I started having sex after about three months. We always used protection but I guess we didn't use it right ...
> 5 anyway Kaylee became pregnant. She told me as soon as she found out. She was crying and panicking and I was shocked. At first we didn't know what to do. We didn't tell anyone and just pretended everything was ok but Kaylee's mom knew something was up and asked Kaylee about it. Kaylee broke down and told her everything. Her mom was great. She was shocked but she was really helpful. She took Kaylee to a doctor and she spoke to me and told me it was going to be ok. Kaylee and I learned about our options. In the end
> 10 Kaylee decided to have the child. It was a boy. He was born in October of my junior year at high school. He was beautiful and I loved him. Kaylee and I knew that we wouldn't be able to give him a great life though. We were 16, we had no money, no education, no plan. We decided to give Josh up for adoption. He was adopted by two women who really wanted a child. They are very nice and they have a great home for Josh. They send us photos and information and once a year we all meet up. So, Josh has a great life and we're still in his life
> 15 but we can grow up as well. It was definitely the best thing to do.

		right	wrong	evidence
1	Kaylee and Austin met when they were 15.	✓		*line* **1**
2	Kaylee didn't tell Austin that she was pregnant.		✓	*line* **5**
3	Kaylee told her mom that she was pregnant as soon as she found out.		✓	*line* **6**
4	Kaylee's and Austin's child is a boy.	✓		*line* **10**
5	He was adopted by two women.	✓		*lines* **12–13**
6	Austin is happy about the decision to give Josh up for adoption.	✓		*line* **15**

E4 Speaking: My plans 👄   ⇨ L p.125

What are you going to do when you finish school? Look at the pictures for help and prepare a three-minute talk. You can take notes first.

How to ...
give a talk
TB p.177

M1 ☀ The Irish Republican Army 👁

Watch the clip. Then answer the questions.

 DVD

1 When was the IRA founded?

The IRA was founded in 1919.

2 What happened in 1922?

In 1922, Ireland became an independent republic, but Northern Ireland remained part of
the United Kingdom.

3 What does the clip tell you about the Catholic minority in Northern Ireland?

It says that the Catholic minority in Northern Ireland did not accept being
separated from the Republic of Ireland.

4 What happened in 2005?

In 2005 the IRA ended its armed campaign and promised to use peaceful ways
of achieving its aims.

M2 What was done? 🔍

Look at the pictures on page 31 of your textbook again. Complete the sentences with the correct form of the verb in the passive.

A The Royal wedding (watch) by many people.

The Royal wedding was watched by many people.

🔍 **14**
p. 104

B The picture (take) in a garden.

The picture was taken in a garden.

C The cake (cut) by the two grooms.

The cake was cut by the two grooms.

D This special wedding (celebrate) under water.

This special wedding was celebrated under water.

E About thirty people (invite) to the wedding.

About thirty people were invited to the wedding.

F Traditional costumes (wear) by the couple.

Traditional costumes were worn by the couple.

M3 Yes, I do

L 2.14 S 18

a) **Listen to Michelle and her friend Claire.**
Then tick (✓) if the statements are right or wrong.

		right	wrong
1	Michelle wants a big fancy wedding.	✓	
2	Claire thinks getting married is very expensive.	✓	
3	Michelle thinks getting married is wonderful.	✓	
4	Claire wants to marry Evan soon.		✓
5	Claire thinks that you need to get married to be happy.		✓
6	All of Michelle and Claire's friends are getting married.	✓	
7	Michelle doesn't believe in true love.		✓

b) **Correct what's wrong.**

4. Claire doesn't want to marry Evan soon.

5. Claire thinks you don't have to get married to be happy.

7. Michelle believes in true love.

M4 (Un)arranged marriage ⇨ L p. 125

Do exercises M7a) and b) on page 32 in your textbook.

c) What can you learn about Lisa's relationship with her family?
Where do you find information about what her relationship with her parents might be like?
Write a short text about what you can find out.

_____

_____

_____

_____

_____

_____

_____

_____

_____

d) Manjit has got a difficult relationship with his family.
What do you think he means when he says he has to 'fight to be seen as an individual'?
Explain your ideas in a short text.

_____

_____

_____
_____
_____
_____
_____
_____
_____
_____
_____
_____

M5 The end of the story 👓 ⇨ L p. 125-126

a) **Read a summary of the last part of Bali Rai's book '(Un)arranged Marriage'.
Is it similar to YOUR ending of the story?**

> Manjit is sent to India by his family. They threaten to make him stay in India until he agrees
> to get married. This is why Manjit finally tells them that he is ready to marry. But on the
> day of his wedding he escapes with the help of a friend.
> After his escape, his family doesn't want to have anything to do with him and he has to live
> on his own. At first he is afraid that they might come after him. But after a while he realises
> that he is dead to them. They even move to another town and behave as if he had never
> existed at all.
> Luckily, Lisa's parents take him in and let him live in her old room. Lisa, who has finished
> school by then, is travelling in the Far East. Manjit and Lisa are no longer a couple but they
> are friends.
> At night Manjit works at the supermarket to earn money. He wants to go back to school
> and take his GCSEs. At work he meets his new girlfriend – Jenny. She has got a part-time
> job and works on the reception desk at the supermarket. She has dark brown hair and
> bright blue eyes. Manjit really likes her and thinks that she is very intelligent.
> After all he went through Manjit is looking forward to rebuilding his life and making his way
> in the world.

b) **What do you find interesting/shocking/exciting about the ending? Give reasons.**

c) **Imagine you had the chance to talk to Manjit now.
Write down five questions you would like to ask him.**

_____
_____
_____
_____
_____

M6 Roles in a relationship

⇨ L p. 126

Do exercises M12a) and b) on page 35 in your textbook.

29
p. 108

c) Use the *emphatic do* to stress these points.

1 I think both parents need to look after the children.

2 You have to keep working to be a good example.

3 I like being at home with the kids.

d) **Make statements about what YOU think about the roles in a relationship. Use the *emphatic do*.**

M7 Nick Hornby and SLAM

⇨ L p. 126

a) **Do research about the author Nick Hornby. Then write a short biography of him.**

_____

_____

_____

_____

_____

_____

_____

_____

_____

b) **Find out as much as you can about the book SLAM. Think about:**
- when and where it was published
- what it is about and who the main characters are
- why it was written
- if it was successful
- ...

_____

_____

_____

_____

_____

_____

_____

_____

_____

_____

_____

1 YOUR future

a) **What would/wouldn't you like your future to be like?**
Make at least five statements.

I would like to I wouldn't want to I wouldn't like to I want to	be famous. have a job in an office. live in another city / country. be active and outgoing. have children. live in the countryside / city. travel a lot. marry when I'm still young. …

b) **What are YOUR plans, dreams and wishes for the future? Write about 150 words. You can use your**
word web from page 40 in your textbook and the sentences from a) for help. ⇨ **L p. 126**

How to …
write
TB p. 182

_____

_____

_____

_____

_____

_____

_____

_____

2 ☾ An email exchange

a) **Read the emails from a British school class to their German partner school on pages 40-41 of your**
textbook. What do you think the German school class asked in their email?

✔ How do you feel about leaving school? What are your plans for the future?

What is your dream job? Have you done work experience?

 **Do exercise 3b) on page 41 of your textbook.**

c) **Tick (✔) the sentences you could use for a reply to one of the British students.**

I don't like Chinese food.

✔ I don't know what I want to
do when school is finished.

✔ I think girls can be car
technicians, too.

✔ Working at the
local airfield will
be very interesting.

I want to buy a car when I'm 18.

✔ I want to work in an
office.

✔ I can understand that you don't enjoy
reading and learning. It's boring sometimes.

3 The world of work

a) Read the emails on pages 40-41 of your textbook. Write down all the jobs you can find.

wordbank
jobs
TB p. 164

programmer _____   aeroplane mechanic _____

TV repair technician _____   car technician _____

plumber _____

b) Find 10 more jobs. Circle them.

N S G H G A R D E N E R V B
U D M L P I K J H G Q A Y A
R N H A I R D R E S S E R K
S B P L M N H T F X S Q A E
E C Y R O O F E R D T H M R
N X Y X C Q W D V R G N Z J
E F I R E F I G H T E R H J
A E S D F G H J I K L Y Q O
P O L I C E O F F I C E R I
O J K L Y X C V B N M Q I N
P B A N K C L E R K F W U E
M L N C O O K Q W E R T Z R

c) Read the sentences. Do you need *since* or *for*? Cross out what you don't need.

2R
p. 101

1 Harry has wanted to become a firefighter since / ~~for~~ he was little.

2 Melinda has been interested in cars since / ~~for~~ she was a kid.

3 Ben has been thinking about his future job ~~since~~ / for about one year now.

4 Aaron has wanted to work with airplanes ~~since~~ / for a few years.

5 Ben has been looking for a position as a trainee ~~since~~ / for 6 months.

6 Aaron has been looking forward to the end of school since / ~~for~~ the year started.

7 Melinda has been arguing with her mum ~~since~~ / for weeks.

4 ☾ Now and then ☽

L 1.11 S 2

a) Listen to Melinda and her grandfather. When did Melinda's grandfather start working?

How to ...
listen
TB p. 174

    1980s

✔ 1960s

    1950s

b) **Listen again. What are the differences between now and then? Tick (✓) what you can hear.**

✓ The work was a lot harder than it is today.

✓ We had less machinery and you had to lift and carry heavy things all the time.

✓ A lot of repairing can be done with computers.

Girls had to become secretaries.

✓ We had to work longer hours with fewer holidays.

The work is more complicated now.

✓ A lot of work can be done with the help of machines today.

We earned a lot of money in the 60s.

✓ There were fewer electrical parts in cars in those days.

5 Jobs have changed ✏️ 🔍

Look at the pictures. Describe what has changed.

train driver

coal • firebox • controls engine

Many years ago coal was put into a firebox.
Now the train is controlled by an engine.
_____
_____

farmer

horses • work in the fields • tractors

Many years ago horses were used to work in
the fields.
Now tractors are used to do the work.
_____

office administrator

letter • by hand • emails • computer

A long time ago, letters were written by hand.
Today emails are sent by computers.
_____
_____

gardener

plan on paper • by hand • software •

In the past, designs were planned on paper.
Today, gardens are designed with software.
_____
_____

6 My English is good enough to ... 👄 ✏️

7
p. 42-43

a) Read again what Jessica and Torge said. Then make sentences about their English.

Jessica('s) Torge('s)	can is able to English is good enough to	take reservations for parties and conferences. read English newspapers. look for information on English websites. talk to foreign guests. talk to English speaking co-workers. get experience in English speaking companies. apply for jobs in English. travel and work abroad.

b) What about YOU? Think about what your English is good enough for. Make at least five statements. ⇨ **L p. 126**

_____

_____

_____

_____

_____

_____

7 Say it in English 🇬🇧 👄

Wie sagst du auf Englisch, dass ...

1. ... du schon seit einiger Zeit Bewerbungen schreibst?
2. ... du nicht sicher bist, was die Zukunft bringt?
3. ... du viele Pläne für die Zukunft hast?
4. ... du gerne einen Job hättest, bei dem du viel draußen bist?
5. ... du dich sehr für Autos interessierst?
6. ... du gerne im Ausland arbeiten würdest?
7. ... du gerne eine Ausbildung machen würdest?
8. ... du eher praktisch veranlagt bist?
9. ... du schon ein Praktikum absolviert hast?
10. ... du gerne weiter zur Schule gehen würdest?

A I've already done work experience.

B I have a lot of plans for the future.

C I would like to do an apprenticeship.

D I would like to work abroad.

E I would like to continue with school.

F I'm more practical.

G I would like a job where I can be outside a lot.

H I've been writing applications for some time.

I I'm very interested in cars.

J I'm not sure what the future will bring.

1	2	3	4	5	6	7	8	9	10
H	J	B	G	I	D	C	F	A	E

8 Describing a picture 🗂 ✏️

Look at the pictures. Then read the description. Which picture is being described?

I can see a young boy carrying a heavy basket of rocks on his head. He looks very young, maybe about 10. It looks like he is in a poor country, maybe in Asia or South America. I think he has to work and can't go to school. Maybe he has to work because his family needs the money. The work looks very difficult and tiring.

9 Child labour or chores 🗂 ✏️

a) **Look up the words 'labour' and 'chore' in a dictionary. They both have got different meanings. Write down the definitions in your own words in the boxes below.**

labour	chore
Employed work that is often physical and hard, e.g. working in a factory, working on a farm	*An ordinary task, often at home, that has to be done regularly, e.g. emptying the dishwasher, cleaning your bedroom*

b) Read the phrases in the box. Which category do they belong to?

> picking oranges for eight hours a day • picking flowers at night for perfume producers • cleaning the bathroom • helping the neighbours • working on a cocoa plantation • working as servants • doing the dishes • babysitting • tying knots for carpets • looking after brothers and sisters • helping at home

child labour: *Picking oranges for eight hours a day*

Picking flowers at night for perfume producers

Working on a cocoa plantation

Working as servants, tying knots for carpets

chores: *Cleaning the bathroom, helping the neighbours*

Doing the dishes, babysitting

Looking after brothers and sisters

Helping at home

c) Look at the pictures on page 44 of your textbook again. Where can you see examples of 'child labour' and where can you see examples of 'chores'? Give reasons. ⇨ **L p. 126**

_____

_____

_____

_____

_____

_____

_____

_____

_____

10 ☾ **Just a number?** 👓

a) Look at the statistics. Then tick (✓) if the statements are right or wrong.

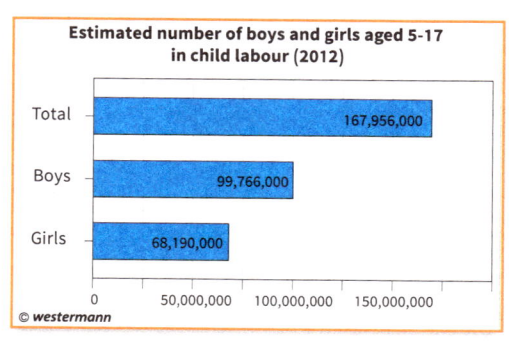

Estimated number of boys and girls aged 5-17 in child labour (2012)

Total	167,956,000
Boys	99,766,000
Girls	68,190,000

0   50,000,000   100,000,000   150,000,000

© westermann

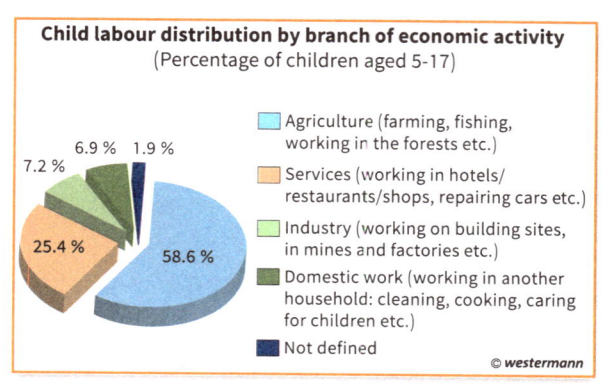

Child labour distribution by branch of economic activity
(Percentage of children aged 5-17)

7.2 %   6.9 %   1.9 %
25.4 %   58.6 %

☐ Agriculture (farming, fishing, working in the forests etc.)
☐ Services (working in hotels/restaurants/shops, repairing cars etc.)
☐ Industry (working on building sites, in mines and factories etc.)
☐ Domestic work (working in another household: cleaning, cooking, caring for children etc.)
☐ Not defined

© westermann

	right	wrong
1 Over 167,000,000 children are in child labour.	✓	
2 There are more girls than boys who have to work.		✓
3 Over 68,000,000 girls between 5 and 17 have to work.	✓	
4 Most children who have to work, work in agriculture.	✓	
5 About 25% of children work in services.	✓	
6 More children work in services than in agriculture.		✓
7 10% of children work as domestic workers.		✓
8 Almost 7% of children have to do domestic work.	✓	

b) Look at the statistics again. Then match the sentence parts.

1 About 58.6 % of children between 5 and 17

2 A little more than 25%

3 There are fewer children who

4 More young boys than

5 Overall, a lot of children

A do domestic work than work in factories.

B have to work.

C work in services.

D work in agriculture.

E young girls have to work.

1	2	3	4	5
D	C	A	E	B

11 Interviewing Ali

L 1.13 **S** 3

a) Listen to Bert and Ali. Why is it a risk for Ali to speak to Bert?

✓ The manufacturers don't want him to.

His mum thinks it's a bad idea.

b) Listen again and answer the questions.

1 What job does Ali have?

He works in a clothes factory.

He cleans shoes.

✓ He sews footballs.

2 How many children work in Ali's factory?

16

✓ 12

24

3 How old is the youngest child?

15

13

✓ 8

4 When does Ali start work?

at 7 o'clock in the morning

at 9 o'clock in the morning

✓ at 8 o'clock in the morning

5 Why does Ali not go to school?

✓ He doesn't have time and his family needs the money.

He doesn't want to.

He thinks he's learned enough.

12 ☾ Bad conditions 👓

Read the article on page 45 of your textbook again and answer the questions.

1 How many children are forced to work?

☐ about 12 million

☐ about 40 million

✔ about 170 million

2 Where does Mira live?

☐ Pakistan

✔ Indonesia

☐ Bangladesh

3 Why does Mira have to do overtime?

✔ She would be fired if she didn't.

☐ She can earn more money with overtime.

☐ She doesn't have to do overtime.

4 What happened when Mira and her coworkers went on strike?

✔ Many people were fired.

☐ They got better wages.

☐ They had to work less.

5 What does Ali do?

☐ He works in a clothes factory.

✔ He sews footballs.

☐ He goes to school.

6 Why does Ali have to work?

☐ He wants to save money for a holiday.

☐ He wants to earn some pocket money.

✔ His family is large and needs the money.

13 Trying to make a change 👓

14
p. 46-47

Read what Angelo, Jess and Tariq do to change the world. Then answer the questions. Give short answers.

1 How long did Angelo and the rest of the band practise for the 'World Day against Child Labour' celebrations?

They practised for a whole year.

2 What did they do between the performances?

They told the audience about child labour and how we can stop it.

3 How old are the members of the UK Youth Parliament?

Between 11 and 18 years old.

4 Why did Jess join the parliament?

Because she wanted to improve sexual health education in schools.

5 How did Tariq find out about the soup kitchen?

When he did a project at school about hunger and homeless people in their city.

6 What does he do to help at the soup kitchen?

He helps with cooking and serving meals, and cleans the kitchen and the tables.

Die Test-yourself-Seiten kennst du ja schon aus Theme 1.
Bearbeite die Aufgaben nacheinander. Überlege anschließend, welche Aufgaben dir leicht gefallen sind,
welche nicht ganz einfach waren und welche du richtig schwierig fandest.
Deine Ergebnisse kannst du mit den Lösungen hinten im Workbook vergleichen und dann deine Punktzahl
eintragen. Fülle dann den Portfolio-Fragebogen für Theme 2 aus.

1 Listening: Linda

⇨ **L p.110**

 L 2.15 **S** 19

a) Listen to Linda and her teacher. What are they talking about?

Linda's grades   Linda's plans for her future   Linda's homework

b) Listen again. Then tick (✓) if the statements are right or wrong.

right   wrong

1 Linda wants to become a hairdresser.

2 Linda's mum thinks that hairdressing is a good job.

3 Linda's favourite subject is maths.

4 Linda's teacher thinks she should think about a job
   where she could use her interests.

5 Linda's father thinks she should become an electrician.

6 Linda is interested in machines.

von **14**

2 Reading: Unicef

⇨ **L p.110**

Read the information about Unicef on page 46 of your textbook. Then answer the questions.

1 What are the aims of the UN? _____
_____
_____

2 What are the basic rights for children? _____
_____
_____

3 When was Unicef founded? _____
_____

4 Where is Unicef most active? _____
_____

5 What does Unicef do to help? _____
_____
_____

von **10**

3 Writing: Your life after school ✏️

⇨ L p. 110

What will you do when school is over? Write about your plans.
You can use your word web from page 40 in your textbook for help.

von
15

_____

_____

_____

_____

_____

_____

_____

_____

4 Grammar: At school 🔍

⇨ L p. 110

Complete the sentences with *since* or *for*.

1 My classmates and I have been going to the same school _____ six years now.

2 I have worked harder _____ the start of my final year.

3 My classmate Helen has been helping me with my homework _____ a few months.

4 I have been getting better grades _____ Helen has been helping me regularly.

5 We have been on study leave to prepare for our final exams _____ two weeks now.

6 I have been thinking about what I want to do after school _____ January.

von
6

5 Speaking: Different worlds 👄

⇨ L p. 110

Look at the pictures. Talk about them. Think about:
· What is going on in the picture?
· Where are the people?
· What are they doing?
· How are they feeling?
· …

von
10

E1 Listening: Teenagers talk

a) Listen to some teenagers. What are they talking about?

L 2.16 S 20

✔ the weekend   their homework

How to …
listen
TB p. 174

b) Listen again. Then tick (✔) the right answers.

1 One girl

   went to the cinema with John.

✔ had to do a lot of chores at the weekend.

   had to buy new trainers.

2 Sam thinks

   kids shouldn't have to do chores.

✔ kids should help with the chores.

   kids should get paid to do chores.

3 Abby saw a TV programme about

✔ Chinese girls who have to work making trainers.

   the rights of children.

   a new fashion trend.

4 The children who have to work

✔ often get hurt.

   get paid 60 dollars a day.

   don't have to do chores.

E2 Writing: Tips for the future ✏

Complete the text with words from the box.
  You don't have to use all the words from the box.

work abroad • university • school • application •
CV • covering letter • skills • special English •
apprenticeship • work experience

If you want to go to ___university___

you have to stay in school after year 10.

How to …
write
TB p. 182

It can be very interesting to ___work abroad.___ You can use your

___skills___ and improve your English.

Your ___application___ should include a ___CV___ and a

___covering letter.___

If you're not sure what you want to do you could do ___work experience___ to see if you like a

certain job.

You can learn ___special English___ for your job at vocational school.

If you do an ___apprenticeship___ you will work and go to school.

E3 Words: Odd one out 🗄

Circle the odd one out.

school • subjects • (job) • study

CV • (listen) • job • application

exam • study • school • (mechanic)

baker • (secretary) • waitress • gardener

E4 Reading: Labour and chores 👓

Look at the photos. Then read the texts below. Match the statements with the pictures. There are more pictures than you need.

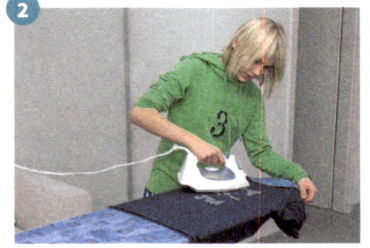

How to ...
read
TB p. 174

6 Many children especially in the third world have to work instead of going to school.

1 Child labour is a big problem in India. Very young children have to transport sacks by bike to street markets.

5 Boys also need to learn household skills, for example making beds, looking after pets and taking out the rubbish.

7 Many kids actually like to clean with a vacuum cleaner.

2 Parents like it when their children help out at home, for example by ironing.

4 Seven-year-old Ajiv collects rubbish from a rubbish heap in the mornings. He earns money to support his family.

How to ...
give a talk
TB p. 177

E5 Speaking: Chores 👄   ⇨ L p. 126

Do YOU think children should do chores? Why, why not? Give a short talk.

M1 ☀ An email exchange 👓 ✏ ⇨ **L p. 126-127**

a) **Read the emails from a British school class to their German partner school on pages 40-41 and page 52 of your textbook. What do you think the German school class asked in their email? Write the email the German class wrote to the English students.**

_____

_____

_____

_____

_____

_____

_____

_____

_____

_____

b) **Make statements about what the English students have been doing and for how long. Use _since_ and _for_.**

_____

_____

_____

_____

_____

c) **Write a reply to one of the British students.**

d) **Do a role play.**
   One of you is a job counsellor and one of you is Melinda. Have a conversation.

M2 Definitions 🧱

Read the definitions. Write down the words.

1 a person who makes things from wood – _carpenter_

2 someone whose job it is to make the wooden parts of buildings – _joiner_

3 a time when you work at a job for a few weeks or months to see what it is like – _work experience_

4 a time (after leaving school) during which you learn how to do a certain job – _apprenticeship_

5 someone who works in the same office or organisation as you – _colleague_

🔲 **wordbank**
jobs
TB p. 164

M3 More about Jessica and Torge

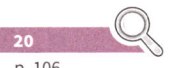

Make these sentences shorter by using participles. Look at the example for help.

1 After they had done a lot of research, Jessica and Torge knew exactly what they wanted to do after school.

Having done a lot of research, Jessica and Torge knew exactly what they wanted to do after school.

2 After she had sent her application to five different restaurants, Jessica was offered an apprenticeship in a restaurant with many international guests.

Having sent her application to five different restaurants, Jessica was offered an apprenticeship in a restaurant with many international guests.

3 After she had finished her first year of training, Jessica knew for sure that she wanted to work in another country.

Having finished her first year of training, Jessica knew for sure that she wanted to work in another country.

4 Because she had collected a lot of adverts from special magazines, Jessica could send her application to a lot of restaurants looking for waitresses in other European countries.

Having collected a lot of adverts from special magazines, Jessica could send her application to a lot of restaurants looking for waitresses in other European countries.

5 Because she had spoken English with so many foreign guests, Jessica had improved her English.

Having spoken English with so many foreign guests, Jessica had improved her English.

6 Because he learned English at school, Torge thinks that his English is now good enough.

Having learned English at school, Torge thinks that his English is now good enough.

M4 An engineer

DVD

a) **Watch the clip and answer the questions.**
   Then tick (✓) if the statements are right or wrong.

		right	wrong
1	Martin's first job after his apprenticeship was as a production manager.	✓	
2	He set up Amdale with his brother.		✓
3	The company is named after Martin's children.	✓	
4	Martin's company employs 50 people.		✓
5	Martin's company produces brake pedals for big trucks.		✓
6	The machines at Amdale are powered by computers.	✓	

b) **Correct what's wrong.**   ⇨ **L p. 127**

M5 New adventures 👓 ✏

⇨ L p.127

Do exercise M5a) and b) on page 54 of your textbook.

c) ☀ **Look at Kevin's CV.**
Then write a covering letter for him.

Kevin Hofer
Hambacher Str. 45
66123 Neustadt
k.hofer@pasvrai.com

Nationality:	German
Date of birth:	15 April 1996
Place of birth:	Neustadt, Germany
Education:	2005 – 2011 Gebrüder-Ullrich-Realschule plus Maikammer-Hambach
	2002 – 2005 August-Becker-Schule
Work experience:	2011-2014 apprenticeship as welder at RSH GmbH in Neustadt
	since 2014 employed by RSH GmbH in Neustadt
	qualified welder, working on numerous projects throughout Southern Germany
Languages:	German, English, Spanish
Interests:	football, meeting friends, travelling

_____

_____

_____

_____

_____

_____

_____

_____

_____

_____

_____

_____

_____

_____

_____

_____

_____

M6 ☀ A child's work 👓

Read the article on page 56 of your textbook again. Then answer the questions.

1 Where do most of the children who are forced to work come from?

Most of the children who are forced to work come from developing countries.

2 How long does Mira have to work every day?

Mira has to work for 12 hours every day.

3 Why are Mira and her colleagues checked before they can go home?

Mira and her colleagues are checked before they can go home to make sure that they haven't stolen anything.

4 Why can Mira's work be dangerous?

Mira's work can be dangerous because they have no goggles and sometimes needles break and injure them.

5 How long has Ali been working?

Ali has been working since he was seven.

6 Where are Sayed and Ayla from?

Sayed and Ayla are from Turkey.

7 Where do they have to work?

They have to work in a dark and damp shoe factory.

8 Why do Sayed and Ayla have to work?

Sayed and Ayla have to work to put food on the table.

M7 Who's the boss? 🔍

30
p. 108

Express these statements differently. Look at the example for help.

1 My mum says I have to do all the washing up.

My mum makes me do all the washing up.

2 Our teacher says we have to read the whole chapter by Friday.

Our teacher is making us read the whole chapter by Friday.

3 My sister wanted me to pick her up from school on Thursday.

My sister made me pick her up from school on Thursday.

4 My dad took me to a very boring museum. He said I had to go.

My dad made me go to a very boring museum with him.

M8 What teenagers would change

Listen to the teenagers. Then tick (✓) if the statements are right or wrong.

L 1.18 S 4

	right	wrong
1 The worst thing for Claire in Edinburgh is the traffic.	✓	
2 Claire normally takes the bus to school.		✓
3 She thinks the local council should try to make roads safer for cyclists.	✓	
4 Sandra thinks taking the bus in Edinburgh is very expensive.	✓	
5 She thinks the council should make bus tickets cheaper.	✓	
6 Sandra thinks politicians often listen to young people.		✓
7 Nick doesn't like the way his school looks.	✓	
8 He thinks there needs to be a bigger youth centre in his area.	✓	
9 He thinks the centre helps to stop young people from drinking and stealing.	✓	
10 Nick thinks the council spends too much money on young people.		✓

b) Correct what's wrong.

2. Claire normally cycles to school.

6. Sandra thinks politicians should listen to young people more often.

10. Nick thinks the council doesn't spend enough money on young people.

M9 Talking about politics

a) Read the website on page 59 of your textbook again.
   Note down all the words that have to do with politics.

voters   _president_

elections   _congress_

vote   _laws_

political topics   _political events_

register to vote   _citizen_

b) Now write down the English words for these German ones.

Wahl – **election**   _politische Themen_ – **political topics**

Politik – **politics**   _Meinung_ – **opinion**

Kampagne – **campaign**   _politische Ereignisse_ – **political events**

Wahlberechtigte – **voters**   _Wahlrecht_ – **right to vote**

Wahlregistrierung – **registering to vote**   _wählen_ – **vote**

1 What are they like? ✏ 🔍

⇨ L p. 127

Look at the pictures and notes. Then make statements about the people. Use the words from the box.

13R
p. 104

> like • love • enjoy • hate • can't stand • be good at •
> be bad at • be afraid of • be fond of

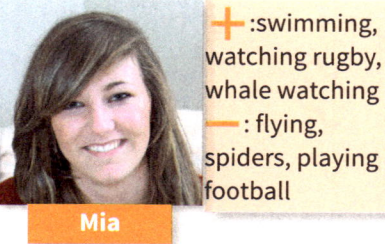

+ :swimming, watching rugby, whale watching
— : flying, spiders, playing football

Mia

+ :reading, chatting, playing video games
— : sports, pop music, snakes

Norman

+ : playing cricket, lions, travelling
— : computers, doing homework, playing rugby

Johan

_____

_____

_____

_____

_____

_____

_____

_____

_____

_____

2 Away from home 👓

2
p. 62

Read the dialogue between Thabo and Isabel. Then answer the questions.

1 What was Isabel afraid of at the beginning?

She was afraid of not understanding people and making mistakes with her English.

2 What is Isabel's biggest hobby?

Her biggest hobby is animals.

3 What surprised Isabel about South Africa?

She was surprised that South Africa has got the strongest economy on the African continent, but also has some of the poorest people as well.

4 What would Isabel like to see?

She would like to see a township.

3 Fly away

Explain the following words in English.

passenger   *a person who travels in a car, ship, bus or plane but isn't the driver*

boarding time   *the time people will get onto the plane*

baggage   *the bags you take with you when travelling*

arrivals   *the section of the airport where planes land and people arrive*

departures   *the section of the airport where planes take off and people leave*

passport   *an identity document with a photo in it which allows you to travel abroad*

boarding pass   *a ticket which you need to get on the plane*

4 ☾ A boarding pass 👓 👄

Look at Isabel's boarding pass.

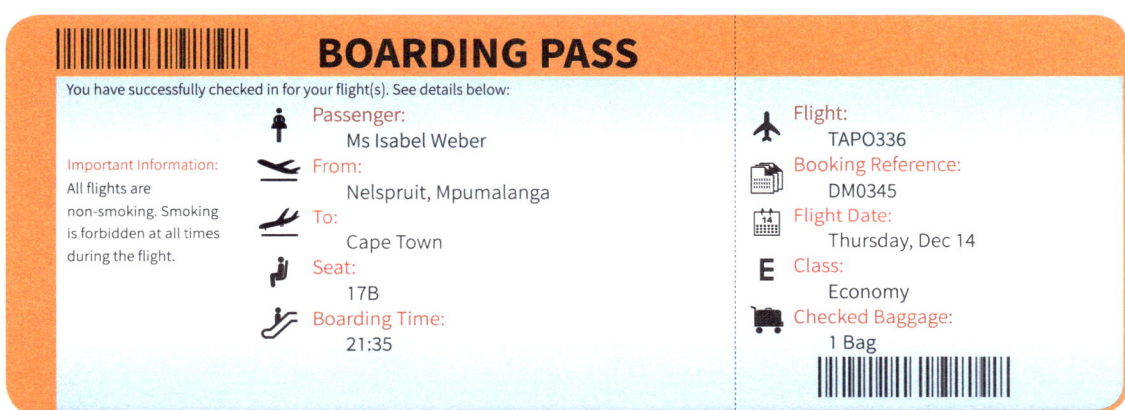

BOARDING PASS

You have successfully checked in for your flight(s). See details below:

Important Information:
All flights are non-smoking. Smoking is forbidden at all times during the flight.

Passenger:
Ms Isabel Weber

From:
Nelspruit, Mpumalanga

To:
Cape Town

Seat:
17B

Boarding Time:
21:35

Flight:
TAPO336

Booking Reference:
DM0345

Flight Date:
Thursday, Dec 14

Class:
E Economy

Checked Baggage:
1 Bag

Match the questions with the correct answers.

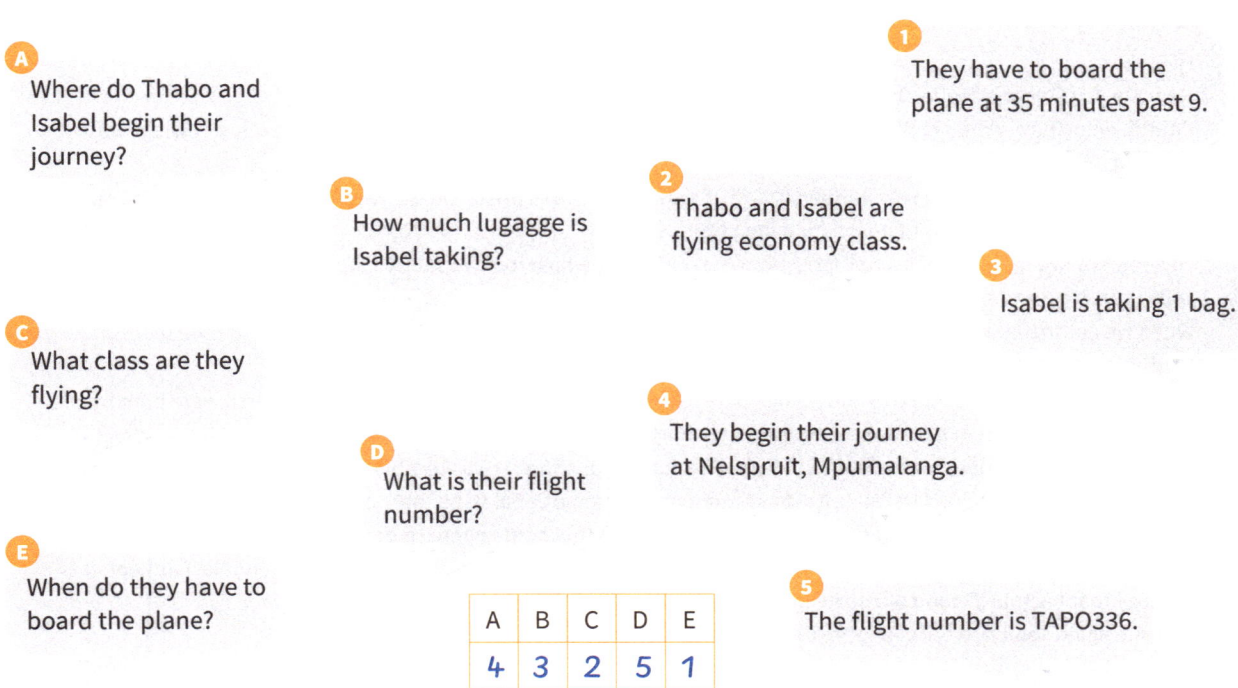

A Where do Thabo and Isabel begin their journey?

B How much lugagge is Isabel taking?

C What class are they flying?

D What is their flight number?

E When do they have to board the plane?

1 They have to board the plane at 35 minutes past 9.

2 Thabo and Isabel are flying economy class.

3 Isabel is taking 1 bag.

4 They begin their journey at Nelspruit, Mpumalanga.

5 The flight number is TAPO336.

A	B	C	D	E
4	3	2	5	1

5 Welcome to Cape Town

L 2.17 S 21

a) Listen to Isabel, Thabo and Baruti. What can they see on their way to Baruti's home? Number the sights in the order they are mentioned.

3 V&A Waterfront

4 Bo-Kaap

2 Khayelitsha Township

1 Table Mountain

b) Listen again. Take notes about the sights. ⇨ **L p. 127**

Table Mountain: most prominent landmark, amazing, great, see Cape Town from above, get a feeling of the layout;

_____

_____

_____

_____

_____

_____

6 An impressive visit

a) Read the email Isabel sent to her friend Gina after visiting Robben Island. ⇨ **L p. 127**
How did the visit make Isabel feel?

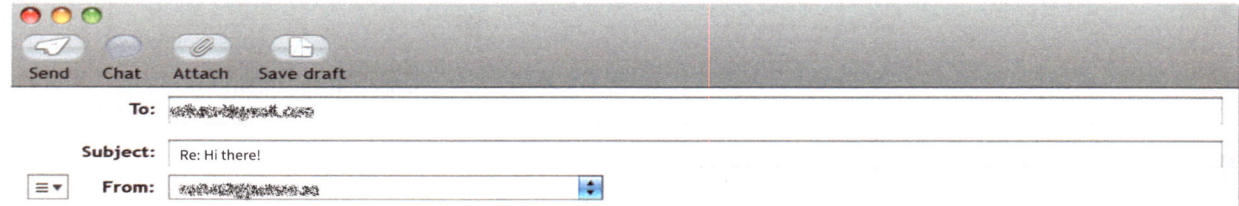

1   Hi Gina,
How are you? What have you been up to lately?
I'm still enjoying my time in South Africa. It's so amazing here. Last week Thabo and I went to Cape Town. It was fantastic.

5   One of the sights we visited was Robben Island. It's an island with a prison on it. It was so interesting! It's the place where Nelson Mandela was in prison for a long time.
To get there, we had to take a small ferry from the mainland, which took about half an hour, but it was fun with the warm sunshine and sea breeze.
When we got there, we were met by a guide who took us on foot to the prison where Mandela and thousands of

10   South Africa's freedom fighters were once held.
The prison itself is really scary-looking. The guide told us that most of the walls and even a church were built by the prisoners themselves. In fact, our tour guide himself was even a former political prisoner! It was so interesting to hear stories from someone who has actually been held as a prisoner. It was terribly sad though, hearing about how hard life was. I almost cried because it was very moving and emotional to be there.

15   The views from the island were amazing. So strange to think that somewhere so beautiful has such an ugly past.
The highlight of the tour came at the end though, when we got to see the cell where Nelson Mandela was kept. It is so crazy that I actually stood where he must have once stood. Not everyone can say that, hey?
I'll write again soon and tell you more of my adventures in South Africa!
Love, Isabel

b) **Tick (✔) if the statements are true, false or not in the text.**

	true	false	not in the text	evidence
1 Isabel has known Gina for 5 years.			✔	*line: —*
2 Isabel went to Cape Town with Kendra.		✔		**line 3**
3 Isabel took a ferry to get to Robben Island.	✔			**line 7**
4 The ferry to the island took about 3 hours.		✔		**line 7**
5 The tour guide was a former prisoner.	✔			**line 12**
6 Isabel almost cried.	✔			**line 14**
7 Isabel wasn't allowed to see Nelson Mandela's cell.		✔		**line 16**

c) **Correct the wrong statements.**

2. *Isabel went to Cape Town with Thabo.*

4. *The ferry to the island took about half an hour.*

7. *Isabel was allowed to see Nelson Mandela's cell.*

7 Working where others go on holiday

 **L 2.18 S 22**

a) **Isabel is back from Cape Town. She is helping a group of tourists to check in at the Kruger National Park. Listen to her welcome speech. How many animals does she mention?**

Five

b) **Listen again. Which animals does Isabel talk about?**
Match the names and descriptions with the pictures.

| **A** cannot see very well – eats ants and termites – is hunted by lions, leopards pythons and hyenas | **B** can be up to 6m high – sleeps only 1.9 hours a day | **C** looks as if it was praying – very large mantises even eat frogs | **D** can be very dangerous – endangered species | **E** lives in and around rivers and lakes – aggressive – can weigh up to 4,500 kg |

AARDVARK

AFRICAN ELEPHANT

GIRAFFE

HIPPO(POTAMUS)

PRAYING MANTIS

A	B	C	D	E
2	1	5	4	3

BASIS Past and present

8 Apartheid 👓

a) **Read the explanation about apartheid.**

APARTHEID

FROM WIKIPEDIA, THE FREE ENCYCLOPEDIA

5 Apartheid was a racist and inhuman political and social system in South Africa. This was used in the 20th century, from 1948 to the early 1990s. The word apartheid means "apartness" in Afrikaans.
In the system, the people of South Africa were divided by their race and the races were forced to live apart from each other. There were laws that kept the racial separation. The system of apartheid in South Africa was banned in 1994. The last president under apartheid was Frederik Willem de Klerk. After this, Nelson
10 Mandela became the first black president. They both were awarded the Nobel Peace Prize for their efforts.
HOW APARTHEID WORKED
During apartheid, people were divided into four racial groups and kept apart by law. The system was used to supress non-white people. The laws allowed the white people to be in certain areas. Black people had to carry special passes or have permission to live and work in particular areas. The government separated
15 mixed communities and forcibly moved many people. Many laws were made, for example: people of different races were not allowed to marry each other; black people could not own land in white areas or vote.
The United Nations did not agree with the South African government's apartheid policies. There were protests in South Africa, like in Sharpeville in 1960 and in Soweto in 1976. The Soweto Uprisings started
20 because black South Africans were forced to study some subjects at school in Afrikaans. Many black people did not like Afrikaans because it was the language of white people and the apartheid government and they did not understand it.
ENDING APARTHEID
In 1989 F. W. de Klerk became the President of South Africa. He wanted to end apartheid. In a speech in
25 1990, de Klerk said that Nelson Mandela would be released from prison.
In 1991, the UN created the National Peace Accord. The purpose of the Peace Accord was "to bring an end to political violence" in South Africa. It was agreed on by 27 organizations and governments.
The first democratic election was on 27 April 1994. Nelson Mandela became president, with De Klerk and Thabo Mbeki as deputies. This is considered the end of apartheid rule.
30 Although black South Africans were granted equal rights by law, there is still economic inequality between blacks and whites. In 2012, South Africa had its first census in over ten years. It found that the average black family earned one-sixth (about 17%) of what the average white family earned. "These figures tell us that at the bottom of the rung is the black majority who continue to be confronted by deep poverty unemployment and inequality," President Jacob Zuma said when the results came out.

b) **Answer the questions.**

1 When was apartheid in place?

    ☐ in 1994

    ☐ from 1994 to 2012

    ✔ from 1948 to the early 1990s

2 What happened during apartheid?

    ✔ The people of South Africa were divided by races.

    ☐ South Africa was forced to leave the UN.

    ☐ Black South Africans had to leave the country.

3 Why did the Soweto Uprising start?

    ☐ The students didn't want to study English.

    ✔ The students were forced to study in Afrikaans.

    ☐ The students wanted better books.

4 What is considered to be the end of apartheid rule?

    ☐ Nelson Mandela being released from prison

    ☐ F.W. de Klerk becoming president

    ✔ the first democratic elections

9 ☾ Gimme hope Jo'anna 👓

a) Listen to Eddie Grant's song 'Gimme hope Jo'anna' from 1988.
What do you think the song is about?

L 1.22

A woman called Joanna who the singer is in love with.

✔ The apartheid system in South Africa.

The Soweto Uprisings

b) Read the lyrics of the song. What do you think the underlined lines or words mean?
Match them with the explanations below.

A Well <u>Jo'anna</u> she runs a country
She runs in Durban and in the Transvaal
She makes a few of her people happy, oh
She don't care about the rest at all
She's got a system they call apartheid
B <u>It keeps a brother in-a subjection</u>
C But <u>maybe pressure can make Jo'anna see</u>
How everybody could-a live as one

Chorus:
Gimme hope Jo'anna, Hope Jo'anna
Gimme hope Jo'anna
'Fore the morning come
Gimme hope Jo'anna, Hope Jo'anna
Hope before the morning come

I hear she makes all the golden money
D To <u>buy new weapons, any shape of guns</u>
E While <u>every mother in a black Soweto fears</u>
The killing of another son
F <u>Sneakin' across all the neighbours' borders</u>
Now and again having little fun
She doesn't care if the fun and games she play
Is dang'rous to ev'ryone

Chorus

She's got supporters in high up places **G**
Who turn their heads to the city sun
Jo'anna give them the fancy money
Oh to tempt anyone who'd come
She even knows how to swing opinion
In every magazine and the journals **H**
For every bad move that this Jo'anna makes
They got a good explanation

Chorus

Even the preacher who works for Jesus
The Archbishop who's a peaceful man **I**
Together say that the freedom fighters
Will overcome the very strong
I wanna know if you're blind Jo'anna
If you wanna hear the sound of drums
Can't you see that the tide is turning **J**
Oh don't make me wait till the morning come

Chorus

E Black mothers have to worry about their children being killed.

C Other governments and protest can maybe make South Africa change.

D The South African government spends a lot of money on weapons.

G Many other governments or companies didn't care about the apartheid system and helped South Africa.

H The South African government controls the press so that they report positive things about apartheid.

A Johannesburg = the South African government

F The South African army crosses borders into other countries to fight there.

J The opposition to apartheid is getting stronger and South Africa will have to change soon.

I Archbishop Desmond Tutu who fought against apartheid

B Black people are being suppressed.

Die Test-yourself-Seiten kennst du ja schon aus Theme 1 und 2.
Bearbeite die Aufgaben nacheinander. Überlege anschließend, welche Aufgaben dir leicht gefallen sind, welche nicht ganz einfach waren und welche du richtig schwierig fandest.
Deine Ergebnisse kannst du mit den Lösungen hinten im Workbook vergleichen und dann deine Punktzahl eintragen. Fülle dann den Portfolio-Fragebogen für Theme 3 aus.

L 2.19 S 23

1 Listening: Benjamin Kau ⇨ L p. 111

a) Listen to Benjamin's story. When was he born?

1965   1976   1990   1994

b) Listen again and finish the sentences.

1 Soweto means _____

2 In townships, there were hardly any _____

3 In June 1976 students and school children started to _____

4 There was a lot of violence _____

5 During the protests Benjamin was locked _____

6 Sportsmen from South Africa _____

7 Nelson Mandela was in prison but he became _____

8 In 1994 black and white people were allowed _____

9 Today South Africa has a black _____

von **20**

2 Writing: Living under apartheid ⇨ L p. 111

What do you think living under apartheid was like? Write a text. Think about:
- where people could live
- which jobs they could have
- school
- …

_____

_____

_____

_____

_____

_____

_____

_____

von **15**

3 Reading: The cradle of humankind ⇨ L p. 111

Read the information about a sight in South Africa.
 Then tick (✓) if the statements are true, false or not in the text.

Visit the Cradle of Humankind

The Cradle of Humankind is a UNESCO world heritage site. It lies 50km northwest of Johannesburg. The Cradle of Humankind is famous for its fossils.
5 Fifteen fossil sites lie in this area. Around 40% of the world's human ancestor fossils, some dating as far back as 3.5 million years ago, have been discovered here. Go down into the heart of the caves and learn about human origins of the entire world. The exhibition
10 centre, called Maropeng, focuses on human evolution and our ancestors over the past few million years. Maropeng means 'the place we come from'.

At the Sterkfontein Caves you can see the pre-human skull 'Mrs Ples' and an almost complete hominid skeleton, known as 'Little Foot'. 15 Although so close to Johannesburg, the Cradle of Humankind has more to offer than a day trip. There are also plenty of hotels and restaurants here if you wish to stay longer. You can explore the natural environment on horseback, pump up the adrenaline 20 on the zip wire, or get married in this stunning location. So what are you waiting for? Come and learn about the origin of our species in this beautiful natural environment.

	true	false	not in the text	evidence
				line:

1 The Cradle of Humankind is near Johannesburg.

2 There are over 2 million visitors a year.

3 You can learn about the history of humans.

4 Some fossils are 3.5. million years old.

5 The exhibition centre is called Sterkfontein.

6 'Little Foot' is the name of a skeleton.

7 You can't stay longer than a day at the Cradle of Humankind.

8 You can get married at the site.

von **16**

4 Words: Definitions ⇨ L p. 111

Read the definitions and write down the words that are described.

1 an area of land where wildlife is protected _____

2 a piece of paper you need when you want to fly somewhere _____

3 a building where people are kept in cells against their will _____

4 a place where you can see fish and other marine life _____

5 something to see and look at when you're travelling _____

6 a political system to keep races apart _____

von **6**

5 Speaking: Going to South Africa  ⇨ L p. 111

Imagine you could go to South Africa. Where would you like to go? What would you like to see?
 What would you want to find out more about?
 Look at the pictures and texts in theme 3 and prepare a two minute talk about your trip.

von **10**

E1 Listening: Life in South Africa 🦻

L 2.20 S 24

a) Listen to Annabel, Dikeledi and Kagiso. Where did they meet for the first time?

☐ swimming pool   ✔ church

How to ...
listen
TB p. 174

☐ theatre   ☐ school

1	2	3	4	5
B	E	A	C	D

b) Listen again. Then match the sentence halves.

1 Dikeledi and Kagiso couldn't have been outside

2 When Dikeledi was younger she never spoke to white girls

3 Learning Afrikaans at school was very difficult for Dikeledi

4 Kagiso went on protest marches and her brother

5 Annabel's son doesn't know what apartheid was like

A because she wanted to be taught in English.

B with lots of people twenty years ago.

C was arrested by the police and beaten up.

D and has a lot of black friends.

E because they lived far away.

E2 Writing: Nelson Mandela ✏️   ⇨ L p. 127

How to ...
write
TB p. 182

Read the information about Nelson Mandela. Then write a short text about him. Write at least six sentences.

NAME	Nelson Rolihlahla Mandela
DATES	18 July 1918 – 5 December 2013
FAMILY	married three times, six children
WORK	anti-apartheid revolutionary and political leader, President of South Africa from 1994 to 1999
OTHER	27 years in prison for his fight against apartheid, received Nobel Peace Prize in 1993

_____
_____
_____
_____
_____
_____
_____
_____
_____
_____
_____
_____

E3 Words: South Africa 🧳

Add the missing letters to find the words.

n__a__tional pa__r__k   __s__afa__r__i   apar__t__hei__d__

be__a__utifu__l__   e__q__ua__l__ity   w__h__ale watc__h__ing

E4 Reading: PheZulu Safari Park 👓

Read the infomation about a sight in South Africa. Then tick (✓) if the statements are right or wrong. Write down where you found the information.

PHEZULU SAFARI PARK is an exciting tourism spot, situated in Botha's Hill, only 35 km from central Durban. The park offers amazing views of the world-famous Valley of a 1000 Hills.
Visit the PheZulu village where you have the opportunity to experience the rhythm of Africa. Visitors are taken into traditional buildings, where the beliefs and rituals of the fascinating Zulu culture are explained. The impressive Zulu dancing with the dancers in their traditional clothes is an unforgettable experience! (Show times are 10:00, 11:30, 14:00 and 15:30)   5
PheZulu also offers a Crocodile and Snake Park where guides will take you on a tour. You will learn interesting facts about crocodiles and snakes and meet Junior, our 102-year-old Nile crocodile. You will also be able to play with Cleo, our 3.2m long Burmese python that weighs 42 kilograms.
Your visit at PheZulu Safari Park includes:
• Zulu Cultural Village Tour   10
• Traditional Zulu Dancing Show
• Crocodile Park
• Snake Park
PheZulu also has a one hour game drive tour. On the drive you will see wildebeest, impala, blesbok, zebras   15
and giraffes. You will be taught about plants in the area as well as experience the amazing views.
When you're hungry you can visit Croctilian's Restaurant. Here, breakfast is served until 11am and you can get traditional Zulu meals, for example Putu – a meal made from maize, crocodile steaks, toasted sandwiches and burgers.
If you prefer to cook for yourself you can stay at our self-catering cottage. Here you have enough room for 5   20
people.
At PheZulu you will also find one of the best souvenir shops in Kwa-Zulu Natal as well as a Swazi candle shop with beautiful handmade candles.

How to ...
read
TB p. 174

		right	wrong	evidence
1	The PheZulu Safari Park is near Cape Town.		✓	*line 1*
2	You can learn about Zulu culture at the park.	✓		*line 4*
3	Cleo is the name of a very old crocodile.		✓	*line 9*
4	A crocodile and a python are special attractions in the park.	✓		*lines 8-9*
5	You can see many animals at the park.		✓	*line 7*
6	You can eat breakfast until 1 pm at the park restaurant.		✓	*line 17*

E5 Grammar: Modal verbs 🔍

Circle the correct modal verb or its substitute.

9R
p. 103

1 You (could) / have to eat Crocodile steaks at the Croctilian's Restaurant.

2 You (don't have to) / aren't allowed to be afraid of Cleo the python.

3 You (aren't able to) / needn't see the Zulu dancers at 5 pm.

4 You mustn't / (can) play with Cleo.

5 You (could) / mustn't buy handmade candles at the PheZulu Safari Park.

6 You aren't able to / (can) take pictures of zebras on the Game drive tour.

M1 The Kruger National Park 👓 🇬🇧

Read the information about the Kruger National Park. Then answer the questions.

THE KRUGER NATIONAL PARK

The Kruger National Park is one of the largest game reserves in Africa. Located in the provinces of Limpopo and Mpumalanga in northeastern South Africa, this wildlife sanctuary spans over 19,000 square kilometres – an area bigger than Israel!

The first area of what would become Kruger National Park was officially protected in 1898 by President of the South African Republic, Paul Kruger. He established the Sabie River Game Reserve, which consisted of what is now the southern sector of the park between the Crocodile and the Sabie Rivers. The aim of the reserve was to protect wildlife from the threat of hunters who had already slaughtered many animals in South Africa. It was an early attempt to preserve untouched wilderness and the

diminished number of animals. During 1923, the first large groups of tourists started visiting the Sabie Game Reserve via the South African Railways. The Railways offered a new tour which stopped in the reserve, so that game rangers could take visitors into the bush. From this, the first idea of a self-financing national park was born.

Not long after in 1926, the reserve was officially proclaimed a national park, named after President Kruger. In 1927 the first three tourist cars entered the park and in 1955 the number of visitors exceed 100,000 a year for the first time.

Nowadays the park receives around 950,000 visitors a year, of which 80 percent are South Africans.

Not surprisingly given the size of it, the park is home to a great number of animals. Among these are 517 species of bird, 147 species of mammals including the Big Five (lion, leopard, rhinoceros, elephant, and buffalo), and 114 reptiles species – including 3000 crocodiles! With a huge all-weather road network, 21 rest camps and 15 private safari lodges, Kruger National Park is now one of the most developed and accessible ecotourism destinations in the country.

1   Why did Paul Kruger establish the Sabie River Game Reserve?

He wanted to protect wildlife from the threat of hunters who had already killed many animals.

2   How did the first tourists get to the Reserve?

The first tourists visited the Reserve via the South African Railways.

3   What was special in 1955?

In 1955, the number of visitors exceeded 100,000 a year for the first time.

M2 Darren's trip

Complete the text. Use words from the box.
There are more words than you need.

anyway · although · nevertheless · moreover ·
unfortunately · surprisingly · however · hopefully ·
actually · fortunately

1 *Although*_____ Darren was worried about going on holiday with his parents, he had

a good time.

2 When they arrived they were very hungry and ___*fortunately*_____ there was a good

restaurant near their lodge.

3 The food was good but ___*unfortunately*_____ Darren ate too much Malva Pudding,

so he felt a bit sick.

4 *Although*_____ the guide Peter said he could not guarantee that they would see

animals, Darren saw a giraffe early on the first day.

5 *Surprisingly*_____ he saw some elephants and a lion a bit later.

6 *Fortunately*_____ there were electrical fences round the camps to keep the animals safe.

7 *Nevertheless*_____ Darren could take a photo of the ugliest animal he had ever seen – a warthog.

M3 On safari at the Kruger National Park

a) Listen to Audrey and Fraser. Tick (✓) the animals they have already seen.

L 2.21 **S** 25

lion   ✓ giraffe   ✓ zebra   ✓ elephant

✓ buffalo   ✓ leopard   ✓ rhino   hippo

✓ snake   ✓ monkey   ✓ antelope   warthog

b) Listen again. Then complete the sentences.

The next morning the safari tour will start at   *4 o'clock in the morning.*

Most animals hide out in the shade during   *the daytime.*

At zoos Audrey could usually see only   *3 or 4 zebras at most.*

On the first jeep tour, the leader of the elephants   *started to run towards their jeep.*

A monkey took a hat from   *one of the tourists.*

To get her hat back, the woman wanted to   *climb out of the jeep.*

On the Tsendze River Audrey and Fraser watched   *rhinos drinking at a waterhole.*

Tomorrow, Audrey and Fraser hope to   *see a lion.*

M4 ☀ Free Nelson Mandela 👓 ✏

a) Read the article about a concert.

The Nelson Mandela 70th Birthday Tribute

The Nelson Mandela 70th Birthday Tribute was held on 11th June 1988 at Wembley Stadium in front of a 72,000 strong live audience and a TV audience of more than 600 million in 67 countries. The concert, which lasted for 12 hours and involved 83 artists, marked the upcoming 70th birthday of the imprisoned anti-apartheid revolutionary Nelson Mandela.

Many people, including the Anti-Apartheid Movement (AAM) and the African National Congress (ANC), believe that by raising worldwide awareness of the imprisonment of ANC leader Mandela, the Birthday Tribute played a major role in forcing the regime to release Nelson Mandela earlier than would otherwise have happened.

Tony Hollingsworth, producer and music manager responsible for organizing the concert, conceived the idea after talking to Jerry Dammers from The Specials, who had written the song 'Free Nelson Mandela' in 1984. Hollingsworth was convinced that a globally broadcast musical tribute would position Mandela in a more positive light, and that news broadcasters would have to stop describing him as a 'terrorist'. He needed the concert to have a ratings figure so large that the ANC and the AAM could use it to show political figures across the globe that the public had moved ahead of them, and if they too applied pressure for Mandela's release, they would be doing something popular with their voters. After some initial reluctance, he convinced many big broadcasters such as the BBC to air the concert. Most broadcasters streamed the event live, under various names such as Freedomfest, Free Nelson Mandela Concert and Mandela Day, but some television companies only showed a censored version. In South Africa it was completely banned.

Among those who performed the songs of freedom, hope, and love were the Dire Straits, Whitney Houston, George Michael, Stevie Wonder, Simple Minds, Eurythmics, Tracy Chapman, and Youssou N'Dour.

By the time of the event, the word 'terrorist' had in fact disappeared from the news broadcasts of the channels that did air it. Fourteen months later, Nelson Mandela was negotiating his release. Less than two months after he walked free in 1990 after 27 years of imprisonment, Mandela came to Wembley to ask a global audience of 500 million to keep up the pressure to end the apartheid.

In 1994 he became the first black president of South Africa, forming a multiethnic government which oversaw the dismantling of Apartheid. He remained a devoted worldwide champion for social justice until he died in 2013 at the age of 95.

b) Read the article again and take notes. What do you learn about Nelson Mandela? ⇨ L p. 127
Write a short text explaining why he was so important.

_____

_____

_____

_____

_____

_____

_____

M5 South Africa and Germany 👄

Look at the statistics. What do you learn about the differences between South Africa and Germany?

There are fewer … in South Africa.

Germany has more …

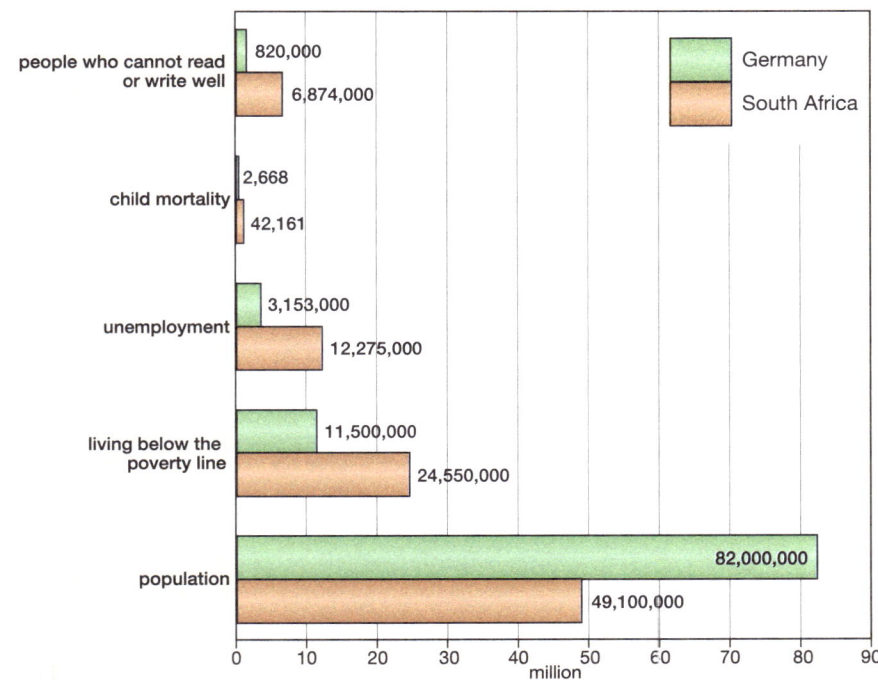

	Germany	South Africa
people who cannot read or write well	820,000	6,874,000
child mortality	2,668	42,161
unemployment	3,153,000	12,275,000
living below the poverty line	11,500,000	24,550,000
population	82,000,000	49,100,000

M6 I love kwaito 👂

 L 2.22 **S** 26

a) Listen to Fenyang and Tebogo. Who says what? Write F or T in the boxes.

- **F** Kwaito music makes him feel alive.
- **T** He didn't like what happened during the concert last night.
- **F** He saw a girl being carried out.
- **T** He says that there were people fighting and someone fired into the air.
- **F** He thinks that there was a fight between gangs.
- **T** He thinks a lot of young people are violent and aggressive because they take drugs.
- **F** He thinks kwaito music hasn't got anything to do with violence.
- **T** He thinks gangs are a kind of family for many young people.
- **T** He won't go to any more kwaito concerts.

b) Listen again and answer the questions.

Where did the boys go last night?	*to a kwaito concert*
Where was Fenyang during the concert?	*at the front*
What does Tebogo know about what happened?	*there were guys fighting, one of them pulled a gun*
What are the kids in gangs looking for?	*an identity*

1 What happens during a natural disaster ⇨ L p. 127

**Write down what can happen during a natural disaster. Give at least ten examples.
You can look at the boxes for help.**

areas • trees • cars • tornadoes • houses • towns • people • news • emergency shelters • meals • beds • …

can be • should be • are • …

uprooted • devastated • destroyed • rescued • flattened • shocked • damaged • lifted off • announced • searched • set up • …

_____

_____

_____

_____

_____

_____

_____

_____

_____

_____

2 The Oklahoma drama 👓

TB **Do exercise 2 a) on page 82 of your textbook.**

b) 🌙 **Choose one of the articles on page 83 of your textbook. Read it, then complete the grid.**

who?	Mrs Denton Luke Denton Mark Stephens Rachel Taylor Robert Deaton 14 injured eight dead	Mrs Denton Mark Stephens Luke Denton Rachel Taylor Robert Deaton eight dead 14 injured killer twister EF-4 tornado
what?	killer twister EF-4 tornado cars flattened buildings were destroyed 90% of the town was destroyed trees uprooted	trees uprooted 90% of the town was destroyed buildings were destroyed cars flattened
when?	last evening 7.30pm on Tuesday	7.30 pm on Tuesday last evening
where?	Lone Grove Carter County Oklahoma	Carter County Lone Grove Oklahoma …

3 Reporting styles 👓 👄

⇨ L p. 127

Read the articles on page 83 of your textbook again. They are written in different styles.
Look at the different phrases they use for expressing similar things.

Article 1
- "A killer twister struck …"
- "… a violent twister devastated large areas of the state."
- "… 25 mile-wide trail of destruction."
- "Buildings were destroyed, trees uprooted and cars flattened."

Article 2
- "A strong tornado hit Lone Grove, Oklahoma …"
- "The half mile-wide tornado was classified as an EF-4 tornado …"
- "… estimated that 90 per cent of the town had been destroyed. "
- ""Not a single building is still standing," he told reporters …"

Which style do you find more interesting? Why?
Talk to a partner.

> I like the style of article 1 because …

> I prefer article 2 because there are more …

> I think article 1 is …

4 A survival story ✏️

⇨ L p. 127-128

a) 🌙 **Write a personal survival story for the Lone Grove Ledger.**
You can choose to write it as one of the people from the articles on page 83 of your textbook.
If you want, you can make up a new character, too.
First answer these questions for your character:

1 Who are you (name, age, job, …)? _____

2 Where were you when the tornado hit? Were you alone?

_____

3 Did you hear a warning about the tornado?

_____

4 Did you know what to do? _____

5 What did you do? _____

6 How did you feel? _____

Now use your answers to write the text. Look at the box for help.

My name is … I'm … years old and I live in Lone Grove. I was at … when the tornado hit. I was
with my … We were warned about the tornado on the radio. We knew that we had to … We
went to … I was really scared and I …

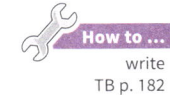
How to …
write
TB p. 182

 Do exercises 5 b) and c) on page 84 of your textbook.

5 Grace's story

L 2.23 S 27

a) Listen to the text. Then tick (✔) how Grace felt when the earthquake hit Haiti.

✔ terrible   terrified   scared   horrible

b) Listen again. Then complete the sentences.

The interview was ten days after an ___earthquake in Haiti.___

It started in the afternoon before ___5pm.___

Grace was buying ___food at the market for her family.___

She wanted to make ___chicken for dinner.___

The market stalls ___collapsed.___

People were running ___out of the houses___ and ___screaming and crying.___

Grace doesn't know how long ___it lasted.___

6 Warning systems

7
p. 85

a) Read the article on warning systems. Then tick (✔) if the statements are true, false or not in the text.

	true	false	not in the text	evidence
1 Forecasting tornadoes is easy.		✔		line: 1
2 Scientists use a lot of data to find out how tornadoes form.		✔		lines 3-5
3 Weather balloons are sent up every twelve hours.	✔			line 9
4 Weather balloons have different sizes.	✔			lines 10-11
5 The balloons carry equipment to measure conditions.	✔			lines 11-12
6 The equipment is very expensive.			✔	
7 Meteorologists use a modern kind of weather radar to detect when a tornado is forming.	✔			lines 20-24
8 Storm spotters report to the military.		✔		lines 38-39

b) Correct the wrong statements.

1. Forecasting tornadoes is difficult. 2. Scientists don't really know how tornadoes form.

8. Storm spotters report to the National Weather Service and to their local communities.

c) Look at these excerpts from the article. Underline the words that are replaced with *one/ones*.

"Scientists don't really know how tornadoes form, but by using what they know about former ones, …"

"Every twelve hours meteorologists send up weather balloons, small ones and big ones."

"By using a modern kind of weather radar, a more reliable one than a conventional radar, …"

"Storm spotters observe storms and learn to distinguish between real tornadoes and false ones. "

7 **Ways to communicate**

Find nine words that have to do with communication. Circle them.

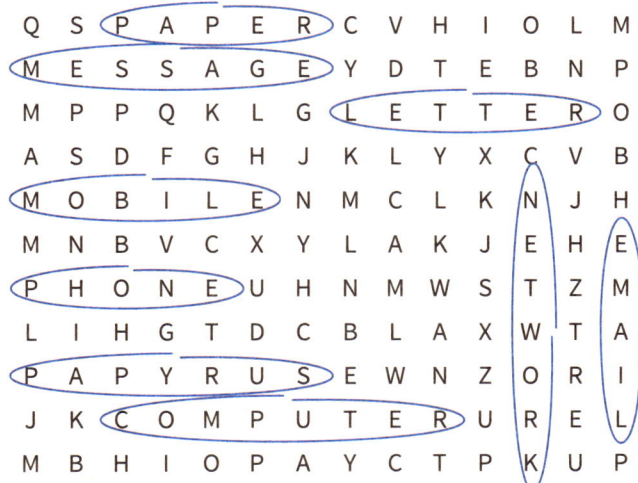

```
Q  S  P  A  P  E  R  C  V  H  I  O  L  M
M  E  S  S  A  G  E  Y  D  T  E  B  N  P
M  P  P  Q  K  L  G  L  E  T  T  E  R  O
A  S  D  F  G  H  J  K  L  Y  X  C  V  B
M  O  B  I  L  E  N  M  C  L  K  N  J  H
M  N  B  V  C  X  Y  L  A  K  J  E  H  E
P  H  O  N  E  U  H  N  M  W  S  T  Z  M
L  I  H  G  T  D  C  B  L  A  X  W  T  A
P  A  P  Y  R  U  S  E  W  N  Z  O  R  I
J  K  C  O  M  P  U  T  E  R  U  R  E  L
M  B  H  I  O  P  A  Y  C  T  P  K  U  P
```

8 **What's a phone?**

Read the statements. Then complete the sentences.

> I love my phone. I use it to text, play, post stuff online and so on. I never call anyone. I prefer texting.

> The only person I ever talk to on the phone is my grandma. Everyone else I just text. I use my phone to find out where I have to go to. The maps app and the text app are my most used apps.

> Talk to people on the phone? No, I hardly ever do that. Sometimes I have to call my bank or work. But I just text my friends and my family. I play games on my phone and I watch videos.

> My parents and my granddad call me. My friends text and sometimes we video chat. That's really cool as well. You can actually see and hear people. Texting is cool but sometimes there are misunderstandings.

> I had a big fight with my best friend because of texting. He thought I was being mean but I was just making a joke. That doesn't happen when you talk to people. But I still think texting is better.

Most people use their phone to ___*text*___ their friends. They don't like

___*talking*___ to people on the phone. They use their phone to find their

___*way (around)*___ and to ___*play*___ games or watch

___*videos*___. Some people ___*talk*___ to their family on

the phone. One person likes ___*video*___ chat because you can hear and see people.

Sometimes a ___*misunderstanding*___ can lead to an argument when you only text.

9 What not to do

a) Listen to the discussion. What is it about?

☐ online bullying   ☐ inventions   ✓ behaviour online

b) Listen again. Then tick (✓) the right option to complete the sentences.

The teacher thinks ✓ students spend a lot of time online. / ☐ most kids don't spend a lot of time online. The teacher wants to talk about ☐ a girl being bullied. / ✓ the dangers of the internet. One student says ✓ she never posts pictures that she doesn't want everyone to see. / ☐ she only posts pictures in private group chats. Helen sent a picture of ☐ some people at a youth disco. / ✓ a girl asleep on the bus. One girl says ✓ you should ask other people before posing pictures of them. / ☐ you get the funniest pictures when people don't know they're being photographed. One boy thinks taking pictures without people knowing it, ☐ is funny. / ✓ is really mean. Oliver thinks ✓ everyone knows that there are cameras everywhere. / ☐ people don't expect to be filmed. He says if you do something stupid ☐ people shouldn't film it. / ✓ it's your own fault. Oliver ☐ filmed an accident last week. / ✓ fell off his bike last week. The teacher thinks ✓ he's happy that no one filmed him. / ☐ it's his own fault.

c) What do YOU think? Do you think it's okay to post pictures of people without asking them? Write a short text. ⇨ L p. 128

_____

_____

_____

_____

_____

_____

_____

_____

10 ☾ How do you communicate?

a) How do YOU communicate? Tick (✓) what you do.

☐ I write emails.

☐ I send messages to my friends.

☐ I write postcards.

☐ I use social networks.

☐ I have a phone.

☐ I use my phone to go online.

☐ I use a computer at home.

☐ I chat every day.

☐ I write letters.

☐ I post pictures online.

b) Ask your classmates what they do.

> Do you write emails?

> Do you use social networks?

> Do you have a phone?

> ...

11 ☾ Online communication 👓

a) Read what these young people say about online communication.

Dara, 17
I can't live without my smartphone. I can contact people and make friends. I don't have to go go anywhere. I don't even have to talk to anybody. I spend a lot of time online, a couple of hours every day. I could probably do better things with my time. Sometimes I think I should go out more often. I should meet my friends in town for a chat or a drink.

Gavin, 15
I use different social networks. I want to see what's happening in everyone's lives. That way I can even keep in touch with friends I met on holiday or who live somewhere else now. I usually write things on my friends' walls. I comment on their statuses or pictures. The one bad thing is that you don't see the other person's face. Sometimes people post stupid things that they wouldn't say to each other in person.

b) What do Dara and Gavin do online? Write D for Dara or G for Gavin in the box.

write on friends' walls G

use social networks G

contact people D

keep in touch with friends G

comment on statuses and pictures G

make friends D

c) What do Dara and Gavin think is good about the internet? Take notes.

Dara: she doesn't have to go anywhere, she
doesn't have to talk to anybody
Gavin: wants to see what's happening in

everyone's lives, keep in touch with friends
he met on holiday or who live somewhere
else now

d) What do Dara and Gavin think is bad about the internet? Take notes.

Dara: says she could probably do better
things with her time, thinks she should go
out more often, should meet friends in town

Gavin: you don't see the other person's face
online, sometimes people post stupid things
that they wouldn't say to each other

Die Test-yourself-Seiten kennst du ja schon aus Theme 1, 2 und 3.
Bearbeite die Aufgaben nacheinander. Überlege anschließend, welche Aufgaben dir leicht gefallen sind, welche nicht ganz einfach waren und welche du richtig schwierig fandest.
Deine Ergebnisse kannst du mit den Lösungen hinten im Workbook vergleichen und dann deine Punktzahl eintragen. Fülle dann den Portfolio-Fragebogen für Theme 4 aus.

1 Listening: Tornado hunters  ⇨ L p. 112

L 2.25 S 29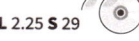

a) Listen to the interview and tick (✓) the advice given by the DJ.

They should go inside.

They should be careful.

They should listen to the radio and ask the DJ for advice.

They should do exactly as they are told when hearing a tornado warning.

b) Listen again and complete the sentences.

1 Dusty saw the tornado _____

2 Dusty took part in a _____

3 They used a _____ to drive around.

4 They had lot of new _____

5 There were also professional _____ on board.

6 They decided if it was getting too _____

7 Dusty and the others always watched from a _____

von **16**

2 Writing: Being social ⇨ L p. 112

Do you use messaging apps, emails or social media? How often do you talk to your friends? Write a short text about your ways to keep in touch with friends.

_____

_____

_____

_____

_____

_____

_____

_____

_____

_____

von **15**

3 Reading: The tornado

⇨ **L p. 112**

Read the articles on page 83 of your textbook. Then tick (✓) the right answer.

1 How many people died in the tornado?

14

7

8

2 When did the tornado strike?

during the night

early in the morning

in the evening

3 Where did the Dentons hide?

in her car

in the basement

in the town centre

4 What type of tornado was the one that hit Lone Grove?

EF-4, the strongest type

EF-4, a killer twister

EF-5, the strongest kind

5 How much of Lone Grove was destroyed?

about 165 homes and businesses

about 90% of the town

25 buildings

6 Where could the survivors go after the tornado?

They could stay with relatives outside of town.

They could go to emergency shelters.

They had to move South.

von **12**

4 Words: Missing words

⇨ **L p. 112**

Use the words from the box to complete the statements.

tornado · survive · forecast · communicate · safe · smartphone · social network · earthquakes

1 Many people who _____ a natural disaster need help to get over the shock.

2 A lot of parents worry that the Internet is not _____ for their children.

3 There are some areas where there are a lot of _____

4 Almost everyone has a _____ today.

5 When a _____ strikes you need to go to the basement.

6 Scientists are always looking for ways to _____ natural disasters.

7 It has always been important for humans to _____ with each other.

8 Most people use at least one _____

von **8**

5 Speaking: The internet ⇨ **L p. 112**

Talk to a partner. Talk about how important the internet is for you.
Explain why you think it is important and what you would do without it.

von **10**

E1 Listening: Marci and Zoe

L 2.26 S 30

a) Listen to Marci and Zoe. Where are they? Tick (✓).

at a school in London   ✓ at a school in the US   at Marci's home

How to ...
listen
TB p. 174

b) Listen again and take notes to answer the questions.

1 What can students use the computer room for? _Students can use the computer room to do their homework when they have study room._

2 How do Marci and Zoe normally keep in touch with friends? _Marci and Zoe normally use their phones to keep in touch with friends._

3 What would Zoe like to use Skype for? _Zoe would like to use Skype to talk to her family and friends in England._

4 Why does Zoe want an Instagram account? _Zoe wants an Instagram account so that people at home can see what her life in the US is like._

E2 Writing: A tornado  ⇨ L p. 128

Look at the pictures. What happened to Steve? Look at the box for help and write about his experience.

Steve heard on the radio that … • He went to the … • He waited until … • Afterwards he helped …

How to ...
write
TB p. 182

_____

_____

_____

_____

_____

_____

_____

_____

_____

E3 Reading: Sterling's story

Read Sterling's story. Then tick (✓) if the statements are right or wrong. Write down where you found the information.

How to ...
read
TB p. 174

Sterling Vincent is five years old. She lives in Port-au-Prince, the capital of Haiti, with her father, Iste Miu Vincent, and her aunt, Elude. A terrible earthquake devastated Haiti and since then the situation in the Haitian capital has not been easy. More than 230,000 people lost their lives and almost all the buildings were destroyed. The town does not look the way it used to before the earthquake.
So when her aunt asked Sterling to go and buy some bread, Sterling could not find her way back home because she did not recognize any of the streets.   5
Pierre France, a young man, found the lost girl and took her home to his mother Rose. For more than a month Sterling lived with them in their tent until staff members of UNICEF (United Nations International Children's Emergency Fund) heard about her tragic story.
They asked the little girl to draw pictures and Sterling began to paint all the things she could remember: 10
her house, her street, her relatives. Following the information that Sterling gave in her pictures, the helpers could reconstruct her way home.
The helpers took Sterling back to the area around her house. The nearer they got, the more excited Sterling became. Finally they found aunt Elude and other family members. Someone phoned Sterling's father at work and he hurried home as quickly as he could. Iste Miu was so happy to have his daughter back, he could   15
not hold back his tears when he held her in his arms.
Together Sterling and her father visited the France family to thank them. Sterling also said goodbye to the UNICEF staff members who gave her a bag with school materials as a goodbye present.
Sterling is happy to be back home again. About 400 other children were as lucky as Sterling and could be reunited with their families. But UNICEF estimates that there are still thousands more who cannot find their   20
families.

		right	wrong	evidence
1	Sterling lives with her father and her grandmother.		✓	line **1–2**
2	Sterling couldn't find her way back because the town looks so different.	✓		lines **5–6**
3	Sterling was found by Pierre France.	✓		line **7**
4	Helpers asked Sterling to draw everything she could remember.		✓	line **10**
5	The helpers found Sterling's grandmother.		✓	line **14**
6	Sterling's father was very happy to have his daughter back.	✓		line **15**
7	Sterling and her father thanked Pierre France and his mother.	✓		line **17**
8	Unicef estimates that about 400 children can't find their families.		✓	lines **19–21**

E4 Speaking: Communication

⇨ **L p. 128**

Look at the pictures. Say what you would do with the things you can see.

How to ...
give a talk
TB p. 177

M1 Chasing storms

Read the information on the website. Then answer the questions.

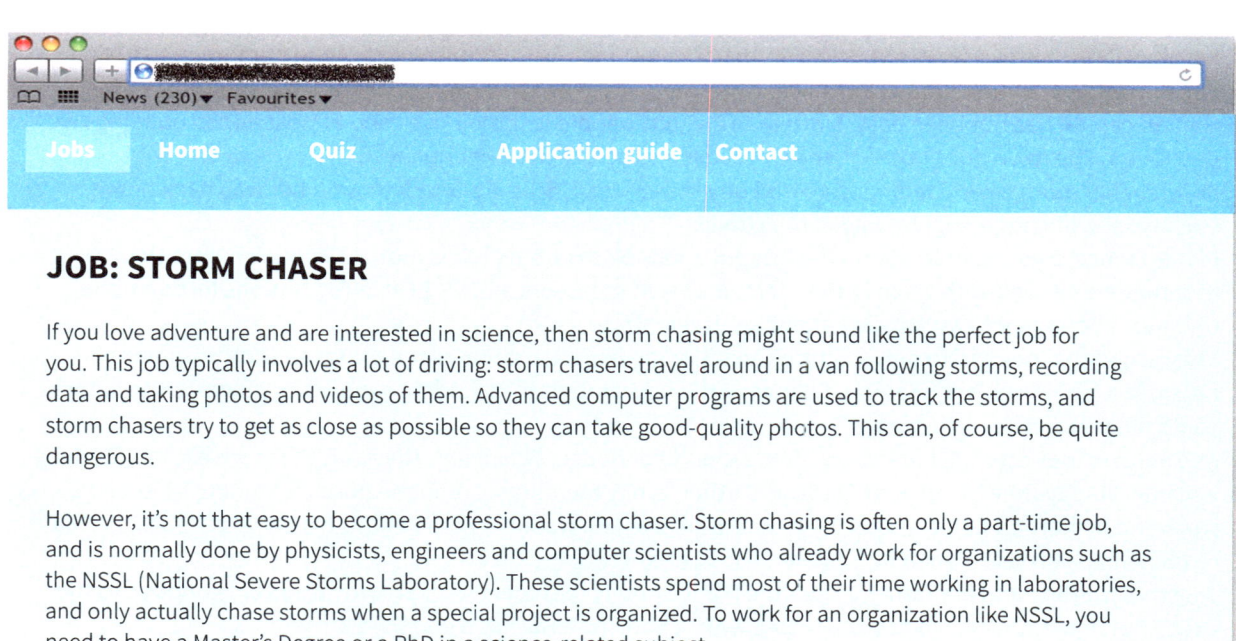

JOB: STORM CHASER

If you love adventure and are interested in science, then storm chasing might sound like the perfect job for you. This job typically involves a lot of driving: storm chasers travel around in a van following storms, recording data and taking photos and videos of them. Advanced computer programs are used to track the storms, and storm chasers try to get as close as possible so they can take good-quality photos. This can, of course, be quite dangerous.

However, it's not that easy to become a professional storm chaser. Storm chasing is often only a part-time job, and is normally done by physicists, engineers and computer scientists who already work for organizations such as the NSSL (National Severe Storms Laboratory). These scientists spend most of their time working in laboratories, and only actually chase storms when a special project is organized. To work for an organization like NSSL, you need to have a Master's Degree or a PhD in a science-related subject.

Some people chase storms as a hobby, using the internet to locate storms and tornadoes and making money by selling their photos and videos. Although you don't need any professional qualifications to chase storms as a hobby, this does mean that you won't earn much money. Chasing storms without the right equipment can also be risky.

1 What do storm chasers do?

Storm chasers travel around in a van following storms, recording data and taking photos and videos of them.

2 What qualifications do you need to become a storm chaser?

To become a professional storm chaser, you have to already be a physicist, engineer or a computer scientist and work for an organization such as the National Severe Storms Laboratory. To chase storms as a hobby, you don't need any professional qualifications.

3 Is it dangerous to be a storm chaser?

It can be risky to chase storms without the right equipment.

4 Would you like to be a storm chaser? Why? Why not?

Lösungsbeispiel: I wouldn't like to be a storm chaser because it sounds dangerous to do as a hobby, and if you work for the NSSL, storm-chasing isn't a regular part of your job. I wouldn't like to be a scientist who works in a laboratory most of the time, either.

M2 ☀ After the hurricane 👓

a) Read the article. Then tick (✓) if the statements are true or false.

New Orleans, twelve years on: a city of contrasts

Since the summer of 2005, the city of New Orleans has gradually been recovering from the most
5 expensive hurricane in history. Hurricane Katrina caused $80 billion dollars' worth of damage to the city, and it is thought that between 1,100 and 1,800 people lost their lives after the river dikes failed and 80% of the city was flooded with water. Twelve years
10 on in 2017, the largest city in Louisiana seems at first to be a normal American city – but one still in recovery.
Before the events of 2005, New Orleans was already famous for its multilingual and multicultural
15 atmosphere. The city celebrates many yearly festivals, and the biggest one is Mardi Gras, where parades of people fill the streets every day for two weeks. Festivals like these were not cancelled during the reconstruction period, and in 2017 remain an
20 important part of the New Orleans lifestyle. At the same time, large events have begun to take place in the city once more, such as the 2013 Super Bowl and the 2008 NBA All-Star Game.
Of course, it is not all good news for New Orleans,
25 and in certain areas, the effects of 2005 are still very clear. In some of the neighbourhoods that were worst affected by the flooding, there are still empty spaces where there used to be houses. After Katrina hit, residents were evacuated and since it
30 took so long to rebuild the city, many also never returned and decided to start new lives elsewhere. This has affected the layout of the city. However, the population of neighbourhoods which were not flooded has increased over the last twelve years,
35 and likewise, hundreds of residents continued to live in the upper floors of their homes while the downstairs floors were repaired. The citizens of New Orleans were determined to stay, and this played an important part in the city's recovery.
40 All in all, New Orleans has become a true city of contrasts. The historic French quarter of the city has brought back the tourists, yet some houses still have graffiti on the walls which were written by rescue teams more than a decade ago. Most houses and
45 buildings have been repaired or even rebuilt, yet some debris remains. The smiling faces and beating drums of the Mardi Gras parades can only hide so much.

		right	wrong	evidence
1	$80 billion dollars' worth of damage was caused by Hurricane Katrina.	✓		line: 5-6
2	More than 90% of New Orleans was flooded.		✓	line 9
3	New Orleans was a well known city before 2005.	✓		line 13-14
4	One of the biggest festivals in New Orleans is the Super Bowl.		✓	line 16
5	The NBA All-Star Game was held in New Orleans in 2010.		✓	line 23
6	All houses that were destroyed in 2005 have been rebuilt.		✓	lines 27-28
7	Some people who had to leave New Orleans because of the hurricane started new lives somewhere else.	✓		lines 30–31
8	Many tourists visit the historic French Quarter.	✓		lines 41–42

b) Correct the wrong statements.

2. More than 80% of New Orleans was flooded.

4. One of the biggest festivals in New Orleans is Mardi Gras.

5. The NBA All-Star Game was held in New Orleans in 2008.

6. Not all the houses that were destroyed in 2005 have been rebuilt.

M3 50 years ago 👓 ✏️   ⇨ L p. 128

a) **Read the diary entry from 50 years ago. What do you find funny or interesting?**

I think 50 years from now we will have telephones that we can carry around. We can call each other wherever we are. I'm sure that it will be really easy to send letters 50 years from now. There will be lots of tubes in the earth so that all the places are connected and you can throw your letter into the tubes and it arrives at the address in a few minutes. We won't have to wait long for replies. I think paper will be different too. It will be waterproof and we'll be able to use it again and again. It will be really easy to call other countries as well. The telephone lines will be much better and a call to Australia will be just as easy as a call to the next house.

b) **What did the person get right about communication today? What did they get wrong? Write a short text about the diary entry.**

_____

_____

_____

_____

_____

_____

M4 ☀️ Online communication 👓 ✏️   ⇨ L p. 128

a) **Read what the young people in number 12 on page 87 and number M8 on page 97 of your textbook say about online communication. How do they use the Internet?**

b) **Note down the advantages and disadvantages of online communication that the seven people mention. What do you agree / disagree with?**

_____

_____

_____

_____

_____

_____

_____

_____

_____

c) Do you agree with the following statements? Why? Why not? Make statements. ⇨ L p. 128-129

"It's obvious that you shouldn't believe everything that is written and said online."

"I feel free without my smartphone."

"I could probably do better things with my time than be online."

_____

_____

_____

_____

_____

_____

M5 Saturday breakfast 👓 ✏

L 2.27 **S** 31

a) Listen to the family. What is happening?

The family are having breakfast on a Saturday morning and talking about how important technology is in their lives.

b) Listen again and tick (✓) the right answer.

1 Why should Rosie put the phone away?

    because they have guests

✓ because they're about to eat

    because she's too young

2 What does the dad use his phone for?

✓ for work and to keep in touch with his family

    to post pictures of his daily life online

    to text his friends

3 Why does Rosie love her phone?

    She can use it to look up facts for school.

    She never gets lost because of the map app.

✓ She can be in touch with her friends all the time.

4 Why does Adam prefer his computer?

    because he doesn't have friends

    because he likes sending emails

✓ because he can play cool games

5 What should Adam do instead of playing games?

    go to school

✓ go to the park to play football

    read a book

6 Why would Adam be the only kid at the park?

    because the other kids are at school

    because it's cold

✓ because the other kids play computer games as well

c) Do you think you should put your phone away while you are eating? Talk to a partner.

Hier findest du den nötigen Platz für deine Antworten zu Theme 5 aus dem Textbook.

L1 Short dialogues

L 2.1 S 5

You will hear two short dialogues. There is <u>one</u> question for each dialogue. Decide which picture is the right answer to the question.

How to ...
listen
TB p. 174

a) At what time does Amy start work?

b) What is Amy having for lunch?

L2 Welcoming the new interns

L 2.2 S 6

Listen to a hotel manager speaking to the new interns.
a) Complete the notes with the missing information.

How to ...
listen
TB p. 174

Length of work experience: ___*three weeks*_____

Rooms for interns (where): ___*on the third floor*_____

Breakfast (when): ___*7 am*_____ (where): ___*kitchen*_____

Working hours: from ___*8 am*_____ to ___*5 pm*_____

Lunch break: from ___*12*_____ to ___*1 pm*_____

Clothes to wear: ___*black trousers*_____ , ___*white shirts*_____ and
___*comfortable shoes*___

b) Listen to the hotel manager again and finish the following sentences with the right information.

1. For breakfast you can have ___*cereal and juice*___. (two things)

2. Interns are not allowed ___*to smoke*___ in the hotel.

3. At 10.30 there will be ___*a staff meeting*___.

c) What can interns learn about during their time at the Black Swan? Give two examples.

___*Interns can learn about working in a restaurant and making up rooms.*___

_____

_____

_____

L3 Teenage mums

a) Part I: Listen and circle the right ending of the sentence.

L 2.3 S 7

1. This radio programme is about
   teenage pregnancies in Europe.
   (teenage pregnancies in Britain.)
   helping teenage mums to look after their babies.
   teenage fathers.

2. The teenage pregnancy rate in Britain
   is lower than in the Netherlands.
   is the lowest in Western Europe.
   (is higher than in the Netherlands.)
   has risen by 20 per cent.

3. 80 per cent of pregnant teenagers
   wanted to have a baby.
   used condoms.
   (hadn't planned to get pregnant.)
   don't talk to their parents about the pregnancy.

b) Part II: Listen and decide whether the following statements are true or false. Tick (✓) the right box.

L 2.4 S 8

	true	false
1 Katie and Martin weren't planning to have a baby.	✓	
2 At first Katie didn't want to believe that she was pregnant.	✓	
3 Before the pregnancy Katie loved clubbing, going out and had problems at school.		✓
4 Katie couldn't pass her exams because she was pregnant.		✓
5 Katie found it difficult to keep her friends.	✓	
6 Katie and Martin are still together and feel happy as a family.	✓	

Thursday

L 2.5 S 9

c) **Part II and III: Listen and decide which statement is true about which mum.**
Sometimes a statement can be true for both/neither of them.
You may tick (✓) a maximum of 9 boxes.

	Katie	Miranda
1. This teenage mum had her baby before she was 15.		✓
2. She had a baby daughter.	✓	
3. She had a teenage parent herself.		✓
4. She is married to the father of the child now.	✓	
5. She never really thought about abortion.	✓	
6. She still lives with her parents.		✓
7. She did / is doing an evening course.	✓	✓

d) **After listening:**
- **What was difficult for both teenage mums?**
- **In your opinion – for which of them was it more difficult? Why?**

Both teenage mums found it difficult to cope with the situation alone. They were both
quite young when they got pregnant and then decided to have the baby and finish school/
find a job. In my opinion, it was harder for Miranda because she was younger and did not
stay in a relationship with the father of her child, or get her qualifications yet.

R1 A sign

Read the sign. Then underline the right statement.

You are not allowed to feed the animals.

You can't eat or drink in the park.

There are no shops in the park.

<u>You shouldn't go into the reserve at night.</u>

Wildlife Reserve
- Please don't enter after dark.
- No smoking and no alcoholic drinks allowed.
- Human food is not fit for animals. Use only the animal food sold in our wildlife shop.

R2 Finding the right course

Read the people's profiles and texts A to D.

Maria left school three years ago and hasn't spoken any English since. Now she is in a job where she has to become better at speaking English. In the summer she has a maximum of three weeks holiday. She wants to do an English course, but she also wants to relax because her work is hard and this is her only holiday. Maria doesn't really like living with other people.

Peter is a computer specialist. His spoken English is quite good but he has problems with writing. He is quite an active person, so he would like to be in a place where things are happening and not in the countryside. He wants to learn as much English as possible and he is hoping to stay with a nice host family.

Victor is an open-minded media and IT specialist. He works on a lot of projects, especially for American clients and sometimes has difficulty understanding them in their video conferences.

He wants to be more confident about having conversations and giving presentations as well. Victor wouldn't mind meeting new people and improving his English in a sunny location but his project-based work doesn't make that very easy. So he needs a course with very flexible learning hours.

A

Do you need English for your job?

Excellent English courses for professionals in the historical city of Edinburgh. Combine a Scottish experience with getting better at English. We offer English for specific purposes, like business, management or information technology. Learn how to write emails and business letters.

We offer a four-week intensive programme with six or eight lessons a day in small groups. You will stay with one of our friendly host families or in a good hotel.

B

Learn English in England

Is your English a little rusty?
You have forgotten everyday words and find it hard to speak?
If you need to improve your English, there is no better way than with one of our courses. Come to the historical town of Winchester, stay with a friendly host family and practise your English. Courses last one, two or four weeks with four to six hours a day. You will be taught in small groups by our qualified teachers. There are also many organised trips and activities in the afternoons and evenings, so you'll see as much as possible during your stay.

C

HAVE YOU FORGOTTEN YOUR ENGLISH?

Take a 2- or 4-week refresher course on the sunny island of Malta and improve your English.

Get better at basic grammar and conversation in small groups of not more than eight people. Our teachers are all native speakers and highly qualified. With four hours of lessons a day you will also have enough time to enjoy and explore the beautiful island of Malta.

Accommodation in nice four-star hotels is included in the course fees.

D

Are you still nervous when you have to speak English?

Do you want to watch English films without subtitles and understand native speakers when they speak quickly? Are you tired of old methods and lots of grammar rules?

Then we've got the deal for you: Book an intensive 1-week all-inclusive course at our live-in learning centres in London or Belfast, or subscribe to our 2-month online course which you can do in the comfort of your home. Whether you spend ten hours a week online or seven hours a day in small groups of four learners – our revolutionary new method and our qualified language instructors will make sure that you achieve your goals naturally – without monotonous gap fills and the usual vocabulary drill. Just listen, talk, relax and you will be surprised at your own progress.

a) Which English course is best for them?

Maria: *C*   Peter: *A*   Victor: *D*

b) Find words in the texts that mean the same as:

• the money you pay for a course (Text C) __*course fees*__

_____

• to make something better (Text B, C) __*improve*__

_____

• boring, always the same (Text D) __*monotonous*__

_____

• out of practice / not as good as it was (Text B) __*rusty*__

_____

c) Explain the words in English.

- accommodation (Text C) ___*the place where you can stay*___

_____

- language instructor (Text D) ___*your teacher*___

_____

- subtitles (Text D) ___*translation of text in a film*___

_____

- all-inclusive (Text D) ___*everything is included*___

_____

R3 **'Little' big help** 👓

Read the text.

1 The Caribbean country of Haiti is one of the poorest countries in the western hemisphere. It has regularly been hit by natural disasters, such 5 as enormous floods and powerful storms like the devastating Hurricane Matthew in 2016.
One of the deadliest natural disasters happened to the people of Haiti in 2010. On January 12 of that year the island was hit by a catastrophic 10 earthquake. The epicentre of the earthquake was Haiti's capital Port-au-Prince. Millions of people lost their homes and belongings in the quake. Over two hundred thousand people died. The shocking pictures of death and destruction went all around 15 the world. Everywhere people were trying to organise help. Specialists and doctors went to help as volunteers, stars like Haitian-born Wyclef Jean, Madonna and Beyoncé performed in a concert and organised a phone-in where they answered phone 20 calls to raise money.

2 But one little boy showed that you don't need to be rich, a star or a specialist to help. Seven-year-old Charlie Simpson from Fulham, 25 West London, saw a report about the earthquake and its victims on TV.

"I just think it was quite sad when I saw the pictures on TV," he said. Charlie started crying and then went to his mother Leonora. He wanted to do something and he worked out a plan: Together 30 with his mum he created a sponsorship form and put it on the Internet: *"My name is Charlie Simpson, I want to do a sponsored bike ride for Haiti because there was a big earthquake and loads of people have lost their lives. I want to make some money* 35 *to buy food, water and tents for everyone in Haiti."* Charlie was planning to do a 5-mile ride around South Park, Fulham – quite a distance for a seven-year-old.

3 With this idea Charlie had hoped to raise 40 £500 for UNICEF. But especially after some newspapers started writing about the little boy, the reaction of the British people was amazing and exceeded all Charlie's hopes. Even with most people just giving small sums like £20 on his 45 JustGiving page, the boy managed to raise over £150,000 for UNICEF/Haiti so far. His mum said: "What started off as a little cycle round the park with his dad has turned into something a lot bigger 50 than that and we can't believe it. I am extremely proud of our Charlie."

a) Find the best headline for each paragraph. There is one more than you need.

1 A terrible disaster   **3** Amazing results   **2** A little boy's idea   Bike race

**b) This is what Charlie's mum Leonora said to a newspaper afterwards.
Put her statements in the right order.**

4 Soon the newspapers started writing about our project.

3 We actually created the Internet form together, but it was Charlie's idea.

2 Charlie came to me afterwards, he was still in tears and he wanted to help.

1 We were watching these terrible pictures on the news that day.

5 From that moment on we had more and more money coming in.

c) Which expression has the same meaning? Circle it.

 **①** to **raise** money

~~to spend money~~

(to collect money)

to give money

to lose money

 **②** ... **exceeded** Charlie's hopes

(was more than he had hoped)

was not as good as he had hoped

was exactly what he had hoped for

was a terrible shock for him

d) Answer the following questions with words/phrases from the text.

1. What was Charlie's reaction when he saw pictures from Haiti on TV?

He started crying.

2. What did he want to do in order to get money?

He wanted to cycle five miles on his bike.

3. What did Charlie want to buy for the people of Haiti?

He wanted to buy food, water and tents.

4. How much money did he want to make originally?

He wanted to make £500.

**e) Decide whether the following statements are true, false or not in the text.
Tick (✓) the right box.**

	true	false	not in the text
1 Some stars organised events to help the Haitian people.	✓		
2 With their concert the stars raised over one million dollars.			✓
3 Most people supported Charlie's idea with quite big sums of money.		✓	
4 Charlie's mother was not surprised that people gave so much money.		✓	

R4 The future is yours 👓

Read the blog.

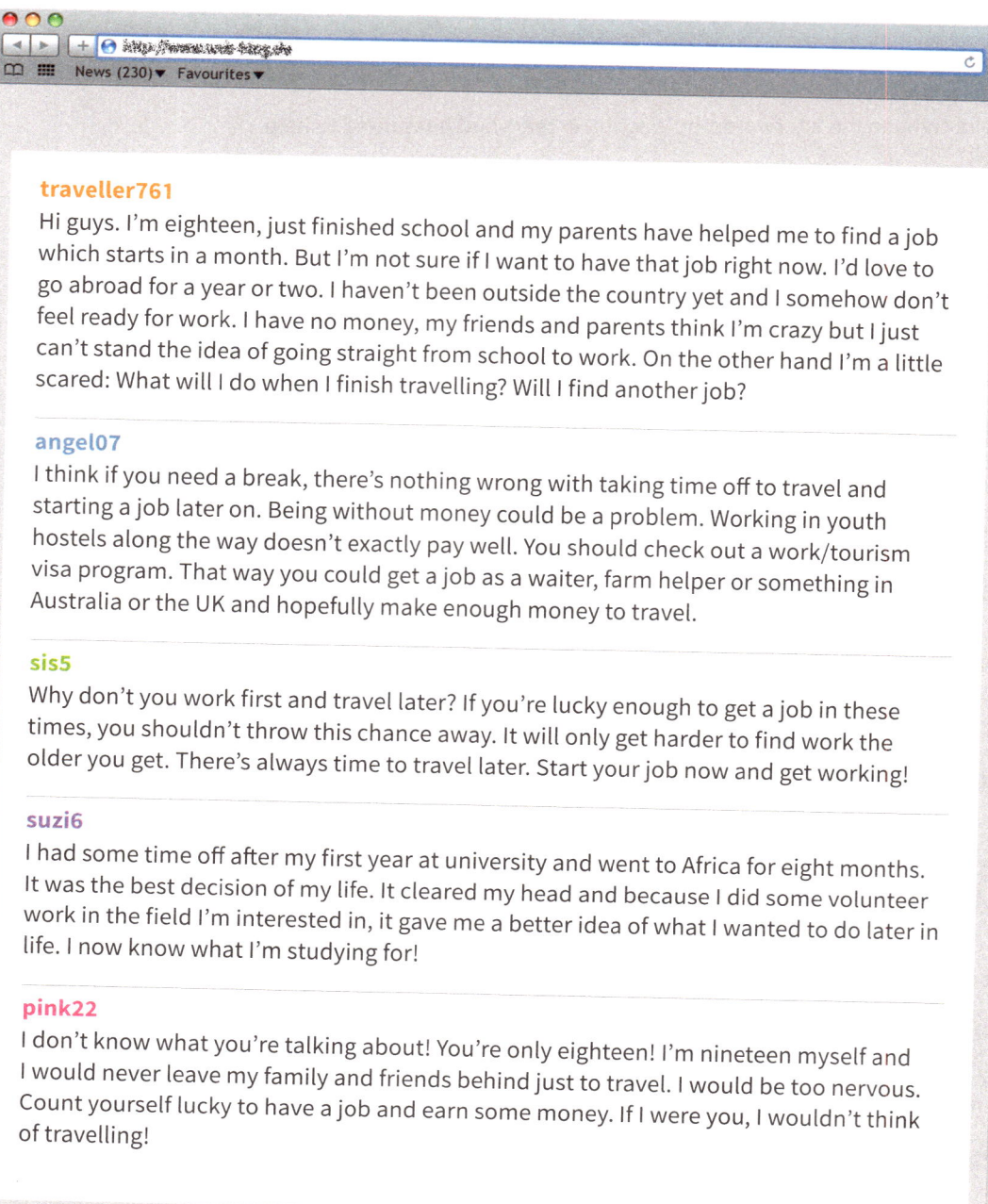

traveller761

Hi guys. I'm eighteen, just finished school and my parents have helped me to find a job which starts in a month. But I'm not sure if I want to have that job right now. I'd love to go abroad for a year or two. I haven't been outside the country yet and I somehow don't feel ready for work. I have no money, my friends and parents think I'm crazy but I just can't stand the idea of going straight from school to work. On the other hand I'm a little scared: What will I do when I finish travelling? Will I find another job?

angel07

I think if you need a break, there's nothing wrong with taking time off to travel and starting a job later on. Being without money could be a problem. Working in youth hostels along the way doesn't exactly pay well. You should check out a work/tourism visa program. That way you could get a job as a waiter, farm helper or something in Australia or the UK and hopefully make enough money to travel.

sis5

Why don't you work first and travel later? If you're lucky enough to get a job in these times, you shouldn't throw this chance away. It will only get harder to find work the older you get. There's always time to travel later. Start your job now and get working!

suzi6

I had some time off after my first year at university and went to Africa for eight months. It was the best decision of my life. It cleared my head and because I did some volunteer work in the field I'm interested in, it gave me a better idea of what I wanted to do later in life. I now know what I'm studying for!

pink22

I don't know what you're talking about! You're only eighteen! I'm nineteen myself and I would never leave my family and friends behind just to travel. I would be too nervous. Count yourself lucky to have a job and earn some money. If I were you, I wouldn't think of travelling!

a) Match the correct sentence parts. There is one more ending than you need.

1. Traveller761 wants to go abroad for some time

2. With the help of his parents he has found a job

3. He is worried about finding another job

4. Although he is eighteen years old,

A he has never been to another country.

B when he comes back from his travels.

C but he has just finished school.

D but hasn't got any money.

E which starts very soon.

1 *D*   2 *E*   3 *B*   4 *A*

b) Which blogger says what? Tick (✓) the right box.

	angel07	sis5	suzi6	pink22
1. This person thinks it won't be easy for traveller761 to find a job when he is older.		✓		
2. This person gives practical tips on how to survive abroad.	✓			
3. This person wouldn't go abroad and thinks traveller761 is too young to do that.				✓
4. This person thinks that you need some money to travel.	✓			
5. This person did some volunteer work abroad and found it very helpful.			✓	

c) Which statement/slogan sums up which blogger's advice?
There are two more statements than you need.

blogger's name:

1. You can work and travel at the same time.   _angel07_

2. Travelling can make you focus on your future.   _suzi6_

3. Travelling is a waste of money and time.   _____

4. Home and relationships are more important than travelling the world. _pink22_

5. Work first, travel later.   _sis5_

6. Volunteering makes you feel better as a human being. _____

d) Read what traveller761 wrote on his blog a few weeks later.
Then answer the questions below with the help of the text.

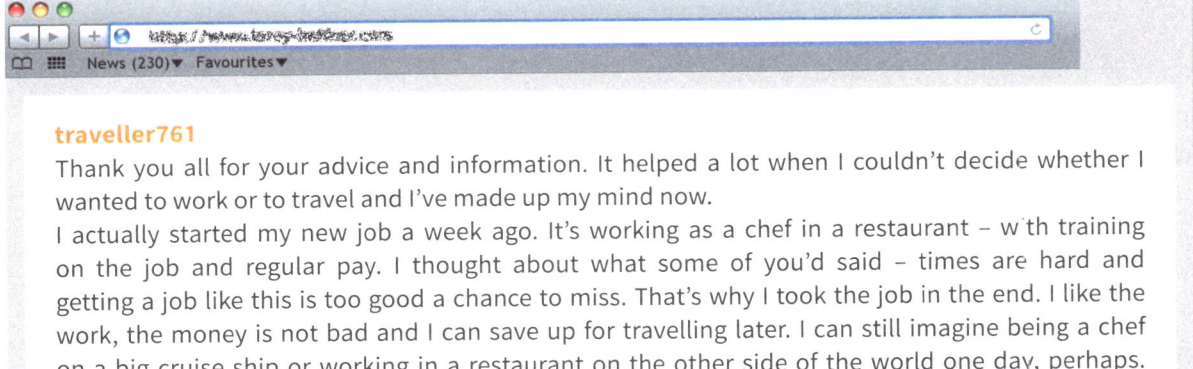

traveller761
Thank you all for your advice and information. It helped a lot when I couldn't decide whether I wanted to work or to travel and I've made up my mind now.
I actually started my new job a week ago. It's working as a chef in a restaurant – with training on the job and regular pay. I thought about what some of you'd said – times are hard and getting a job like this is too good a chance to miss. That's why I took the job in the end. I like the work, the money is not bad and I can save up for travelling later. I can still imagine being a chef on a big cruise ship or working in a restaurant on the other side of the world one day, perhaps.

1. What are traveller761's reasons for taking the job?

He took the job because he knows it is difficult to find a job at the moment, so he

shouldn't say no to such a chance. He can still travel later.

2. What tells you that he has not given up his dream of travelling?

He would like to become a chef on a cruise ship or work somewhere else in the world,

far away.

W1 A form

You have travelled from Berlin to London to go on an English course. When you arrive at Heathrow Airport, they have lost your luggage. Now you have to fill in this form to get it back. Give the information asked for.

Lösungsbeispiel:

first name: **Lars**	surname: **Walter**
sex: ☑ male ☐ female	nationality: **German**
home address (including country): **Mehringdamm 72** **13358 Berlin** **Germany**	
age: **16**	airport of departure: **Berlin**
final destination: **Manchester**	length of stay in Britain: **two weeks**
contact telephone number in Britain (mobile or landline): **0044-7746-5356975**	
type of accommodation in Britain: **private**	purpose of trip: **English course**
content of luggage (2 things): **red trainers (Converse)** **book: 'English for beginners'**	description of luggage (2 details): **1 large black suitcase** **1 blue rucksack**
estimated value of luggage and contents (in €): **850**	signature: **Lars Walter**

W2 Reacting to a comment ✎

**You have posted this photo online. Your friend Max wants to know more about it.
React to his comment and answer his questions. Write a text for the photo.**

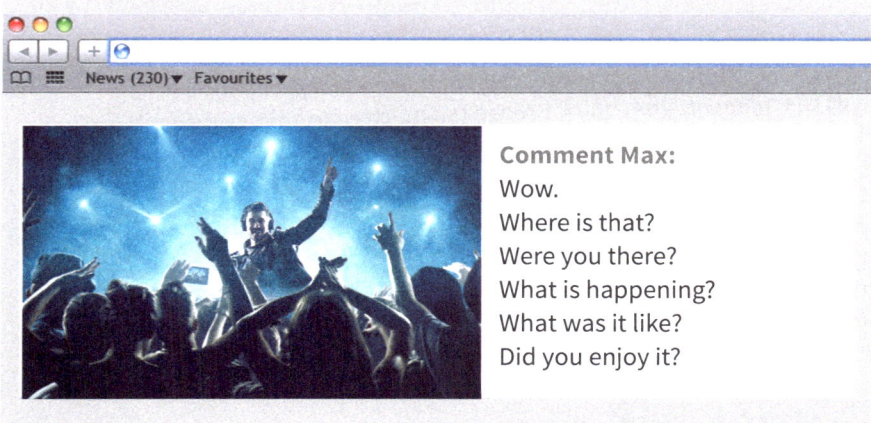

> **Comment Max:**
> Wow.
> Where is that?
> Were you there?
> What is happening?
> What was it like?
> Did you enjoy it?

Lösungsbeispiel:

Hey Max!

Yeah, I was there! The singer came right up to us to sing the chorus. It was amazing —

I loved every second of it. This was at the O2 Arena in Greenwich, in South-East London.

It was the best night of my whole life!

W3 Writing a complaint ✎

**Four weeks ago you ordered and paid for a pair of expensive American trainers on a US website. The
trainers still haven't arrived. Write an email or a formal letter to the American supplier in which you**

- tell them what you ordered
- say when you ordered it
- inform them what you paid
- give them a deadline by which to deliver or ask for your money back

Lösungsbeispiel:

To whom it may concern,

I recently ordered a pair of expensive trainers from your website and have been waiting

for them for three weeks, so since April. The trainers cost 200 dollars, as well as

25 dollars for delivery. Therefore, I am sure you can understand my annoyance.

I ordered the trainers in order to wear them on holiday at the beginning of June, so I

expect to have them by the end of this month at the latest. If this will prove to be a

problem, let me know immediately so that I can expect a refund.

Many thanks, Catherine Roberts

W4 Answering a letter / an email / a blog entry ✏

Read the two texts. Then choose one of them and answer it.

2nd March 20..

Dear ...,

Sorry I haven't written to you for ages but I'm having real problems with my parents at the moment. They think I spend too much time online and don't work hard enough in school.
So they only let me use my smartphone for half an hour a day. They have also banned me from using any social networking sites because they think it's too dangerous. Do you have similar problems with your parents? Have you got any ideas what I could do?
How can I explain to them how important online social networking and my smartphone are to me?
Please write back soon.

Yours,
Matthew

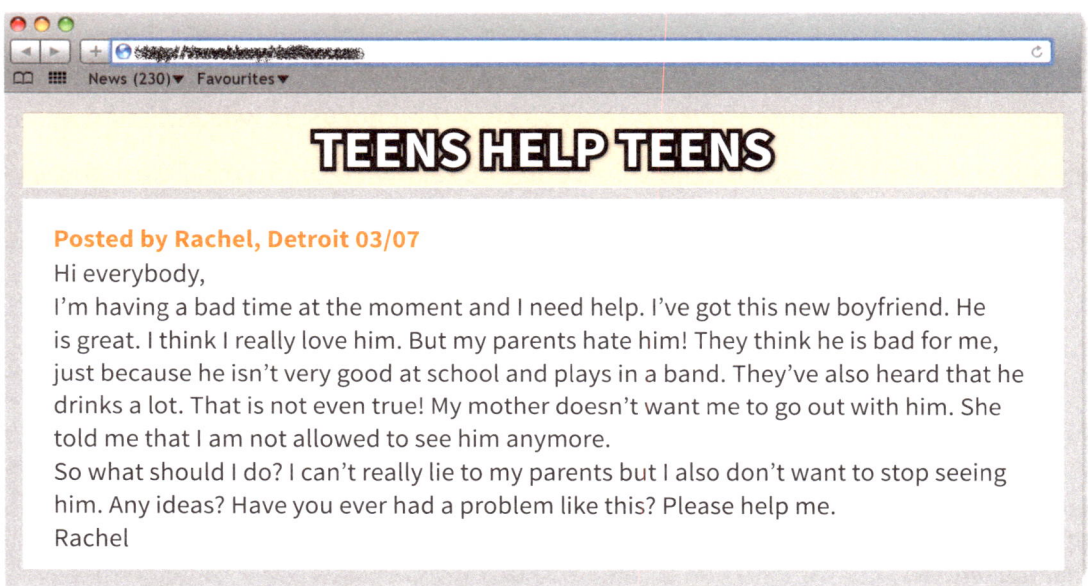

TEENS HELP TEENS

Posted by Rachel, Detroit 03/07

Hi everybody,
I'm having a bad time at the moment and I need help. I've got this new boyfriend. He is great. I think I really love him. But my parents hate him! They think he is bad for me, just because he isn't very good at school and plays in a band. They've also heard that he drinks a lot. That is not even true! My mother doesn't want me to go out with him. She told me that I am not allowed to see him anymore.
So what should I do? I can't really lie to my parents but I also don't want to stop seeing him. Any ideas? Have you ever had a problem like this? Please help me.
Rachel

Lösungsbeispiel:

Dear Matthew,

Thanks for your letter — and don't worry about not writing earlier. I understand your

problem, I've had the same discussions with my parents again and again.

But it got better after our 'official agreement'. We actually wrote it down and signed it.

My parents agreed that they would at least have a look at the sites I visit because I

found it really unfair that they didn't allow things they didn't even know about. They

also agreed on 'school computer time' and 'private computer time'.

And the last point we wrote down is that I'm allowed to use the computer for half an

hour a day but that I can save up that time. So, when I've got an important exam, I spend _more time learning for school and less on the computer but then I can use my complete_

computer time in one go.

And guess what? My grades got better. And we argue less.

Maybe you could suggest something similar to your parents? I mean, when they see that

you are willing to find a solution, they might be a bit more tolerant as well. Good luck!

Yours,

Alexander

Dear Rachel, ⇨ **L p. 129**

W5 **A flyer or a poster** ✎

a) **You are on an exchange visit at an English school and have lost your mobile phone there. Write the text for a flyer/poster/notice that you can put on the information board. On the flyer/poster/notice you should say**

- what it is about
- where and when you think you lost the mobile
- what kind of mobile it is/what it looks like
  Ask everybody to help you find it.

- your contact details
- if there is any reward for the person who gets it back to you

Lösungsbeispiel:

MOBILE PHOHE LOST —

HOT CHOCOLATE OR COFFEE AS REWARD FOR RETURN

I lost my BLACK NOKIA 6235 last Thursday,

probably in cafteria or gym (but could have been somewhere else).

If anyone finds it, please call me on 592588 or email me at littlemisssunshine@web.com

b) **As part of an English project you are organising a film evening about teenage relationships. Write a text for a poster for the event. Say**

- which film(s) you are going to show
- when and where it is going to be

- who can come
- what people should bring

Lösungsbeispiel:

FILM EVENING

12 October — 8 pm —biology lab — admission free

See Ellen Page in JUNO — a US film about a teenage pregnancy.

Everyone over 6 can come.

Please bring your own chair — there may not be enough room for everyone.

W6 Creative writing ✎

Choose one topic, tick (✔) it and write a text.

1. Write a report about some work experience or an after-school job that you have done. Talk about what you did, the things you learned and what you liked/didn't like about this experience.
2. How do you imagine 'The perfect wedding'? Write a personal article for the magazine 'Teenage Bride'.
3. Your home town/area wants to attract more foreign tourists. You were asked to help with the English website. Write a text for this website. Describe the attractions of your home town/ area, things to do and other things that might interest foreign tourists (food, nightlife, etc.).
4. You have just returned from your final class trip / a day out with your class at the end of tenth grade. Write a diary entry about what you did, where you went, what happened and how you felt.
5. Write a story. Choose one of the following titles:
   How I won the prize • The visitor • What a day! • Truth and lies • Saved!
6. Use these pictures to write a story:

Lösungsbeispiel:

1. The world of work

I did my work experience in the office where my aunt works. She is an administrative assistant in a company that produces cars.

I helped with sending out letters, answering the phone, making coffee, sorting files and I cleaned up the storage room. I liked all the people who work in the office, they were very friendly.

I also liked sorting files because I learned a lot about office organization.

I did not like cleaning the storage room. It was really dirty in there. Also, there were some really heavy boxes and the shelves were really high. I spent three days on a ladder in clouds of dust.

And I did not like that I was on my own in there. It was boring because I had nobody to talk to. But in the end the room looked much nicer. It was a good feeling to see the result of my hard work.

Lösungsbeispiele 2 – 6:   ⇨ **L p. 129-130**

W7 Discussing statements

**Choose one of the following statements, tick (✓) it and write down your opinion.
Give reasons for your opinion using examples where possible.**

1. Parents shouldn't worry about social networking sites because these sites
   are an important part of teenage communication.
2. In our modern world you can't survive without a computer
   and a mobile phone.
3. Life for teenagers today is much easier than it was
   thirty years ago.
4. Every teenager should do some volunteer work after
   finishing school.
5. It is best for young people to take time out after school and
   travel to see the world.
6. It is best to have children early in life because then you are
   fit and active enough for them.

Lösungsbeispiel:

1. Thousands of teenagers use social networking sites every day to stay in touch. Some
parents worry that these sites are dangerous for their children, but others disagree,
saying that it is a good way to communicate.

In my opinion, parents needn't worry if their child is sensible. A lot of people have
friends who they can't see because they go to different schools or live in different
towns or even countries. Social networking sites allow them to talk to each other
and share photos and videos easily.

On the other hand, many teenagers spend more time using these sites than talking to
their family or friends, which is damaging for social interaction. Some people also use
the Internet to find out personal information about other people, which they then use
for crimes.

All in all, however, I think that social networking sites are safe, as long as you don't
use them too much and put personal information online.   (158 words)

Lösungsbeispiele 2 – 6:   ⇨ **L p. 130-131**

MD1 Choosing a present 🇬🇧

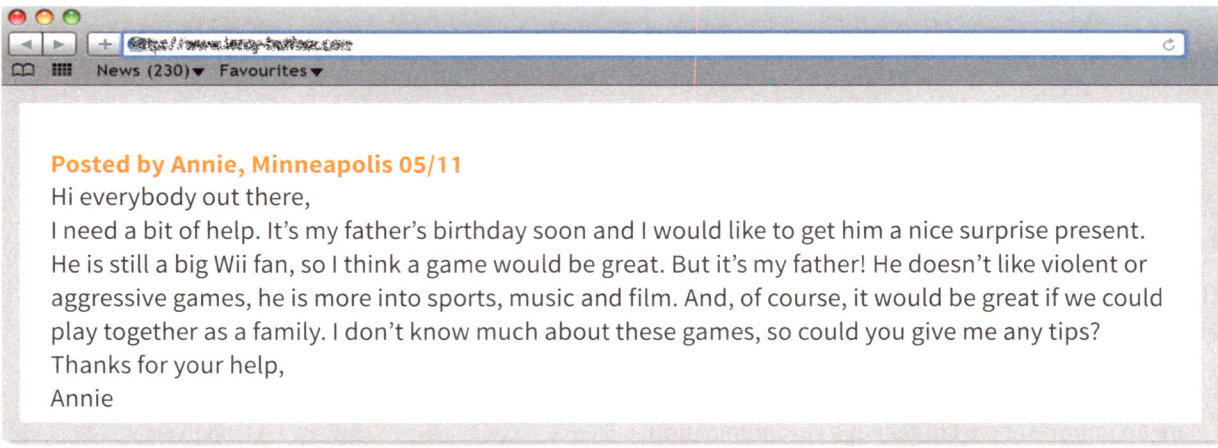

Posted by Annie, Minneapolis 05/11
Hi everybody out there,
I need a bit of help. It's my father's birthday soon and I would like to get him a nice surprise present.
He is still a big Wii fan, so I think a game would be great. But it's my father! He doesn't like violent or
aggressive games, he is more into sports, music and film. And, of course, it would be great if we could
play together as a family. I don't know much about these games, so could you give me any tips?
Thanks for your help,
Annie

You have read Annie's message in a chat room and have found these two games. Choose one of them and write an answer to her in English. Tell her what kind of game it is and why you think it would be a good present for her father.

Family Party Winter Fun
bringt die ganze Familie an die Wii. Es bietet einen unterhaltsamen Mix aus verschiedenen traditionellen Wintersportarten und winterlichen Aktivitäten. Mit Sicherheit ist für jedes Familienmitglied etwas dabei. Bei über dreißig verschiedenen Minispielen wie Skifahren, Snowboarden, Hundeschlittenrennen, Schneeballschlachten, Eislaufen usw. kann keine Langeweile aufkommen. Family Party Winter Fun erlaubt das gleichzeitige Agieren mehrerer Spieler und ist für alle Altersgruppen geeignet.

Let's Sing
sorgt für jede Menge Spaß und hat coole Spielvarianten dabei. Im Solo-Modus singst du alleine oder trainierst deine Fähigkeiten. Gemeinsam ist es doch am schönsten: Sing mit Freunden ein Duett oder liefert zusammen im Koop-Modus die beste Performance ab. Im Battle-Modus findet ihr heraus, wer der bessere Sänger ist. Du kennst deinen Lieblingshit auswendig? Dann beweise es im „Aus dem Kopf"-Modus, in dem nach und nach der Text verschwindet – oder sogar ganz ohne Musik, a cappella. Du hast die Wahl. Es stehen dir über 30 internationale Chart-Hits zur Verfügung. Diese können entweder im Singleplayer- oder im Multiplayer-Modus mit bis zu vier Spielern nachgesungen werden.

Lösungsbeispiel: (Family Party Winter Fun)

Hi Annie,

I think I know a game that your father will love. It's a winter sports game for the whole

family so you can all enjoy it with him. When you play Family Party Winter Fun, you can

try any of the thirty different traditional winter sports and activities. So everybody will

find something they like. You can try skiing, snowboarding or even have snowball fights,

so I don't think you'll get bored!

Also, more than one person can play at once and it says people of any age can play, so get

your grandparents to play, too!

Hope that helps, Jess

Lösungsbeispiel: (Let's Sing)   ⇨ **L p. 131**

MD2 Important information

**You are on holiday with your parents in Florida and you come across this sign.
Tell your parents what it is about and give them the most important information in German.**

Caution Alligators!

- No swimming in this area.
- Only swim in designated areas protected by lifeguards.
- Don't go too close to the edge of the water.
- Do not feed or molest any alligators. They prefer hands to handouts.
- Be especially watchful at dawn or dusk and at night.
- Alligator sightings should be reported to our park rangers by calling freephone 566-911-6600.

Hier gibt's Alligatoren.

Schwimmen ist nur in gekennzeichneten Gebieten erlaubt.

Wir sollen nicht zu nah ans Wasser gehen, vor allem nicht abends oder nachts.

Wenn wir ein Alligator sehen, sollten wir den Ranger anrufen, das hier ist die Telefonnummer.

Außerdem sollen wir Alligatoren nicht füttern oder ärgern.

MD3 In a tourist information office

**You are on holiday in Cape Town. In a tourist information office you notice an elderly German couple.
They need some information and have problems with English. You offer to help them. Put the most
important information into English/German for them.**

German couple: Wir würden gern zum Table Mountain und brauchen ein paar Informationen.

You: *They would like to go to Table Mountain and need some information about it.*

Tourist office clerk: There is the Table Mountain Aerial Cableway. This is the best way to get a good view. You can see the whole of Cape Town.

You: *Es gibt die Table-Mountain-Seilbahn. Mit der Seilbahn hat man den besten Ausblick. Man kann ganz Kapstadt sehen.*

German couple: Was für eine Seilbahn ist denn das?

You: *What kind of cableway is it?*

Tourist office clerk: These cable cars have huge windows and the floor rotates so that visitors get the full 360 degree view of the fantastic scenery.

You: *Die Seilbahnen haben große Fenster und der Boden dreht sich. So hat man einen kompletten 360-Grad-Rundblick.*

German couple: Das hört sich toll an. Dauert die Fahrt denn lange?

You: *That sounds great. They would like to know how long it takes.*

Tourist office clerk: It takes less than ten minutes to the top of Table Mountain.

You: *Weniger als zehn Minuten bis nach oben.*

German couple: Hm. Das ist bestimmt teuer. Wie viel

kostet denn die Fahrt mit der Seilbahn?

You: <u>How much is it? / How much does it cost to take the cable car?</u>

Tourist office clerk: If you go in the morning, the return ticket for adults is 285 rand. From 1 pm onwards the return ticket is 255 rand.

You: <u>Vormittags koste eine Fahrkarte für Ewachsene, hin und zurück, 285 Rand. Ab 13 Uhr kostet dieselbe Fahrkarte 255 Rand.</u>

German couple: Das geht ja. Dann werden wir wohl

nach dem Mittagessen fahren. Vielen Dank für die Hilfe!

You (to the tourist office clerk): Thank you!

Tourist office clerk: Oh, by the way, tell them they should take a jacket. It might be hot down here but up there it can get cool.

You: <u>Denken Sie daran, eine Jacke mitzunehmen. Es kann da oben kalt sein.</u>

German couple: Thank you!

LG1 About *Juno*

Read the text. Some words or expressions are missing. Circle them in the chart below.

Juno is a film about a teenage girl who (1) pregnant and knows she doesn't want to keep the baby. Juno's parents are shocked when she (2) them at first but then they support (3) daughter and her decision with a lot of warmth and understanding. She decides to give her baby up for adoption and starts looking (4) a nice family. She finds Vanessa and Mark, (5) seem to be a nice couple. During her pregnancy Juno begins to form a (6) friendship with Mark (7) they are both interested in horror films and punk music.

1	is getting	(gets)	was	get
2	speaks	talks	(tells)	says
3	there	her	they're	(their)
4	up	after	(for)	at
5	(who)	which	whose	they
6	near	(close)	nearly	best
7	(because)	when	then	although

LG2 Teenage pregnancy

Read the sentences. Then complete the second sentence of each pair so that it means the same as the first.

1. The rate of teenage pregnancies in England and Wales has dropped a lot since 2007. –

   In 2007, the rate of teenage pregnancies in England and Wales was <u>*higher*</u>.

2. The teenage pregnancy rate in Britain is still higher than in any other country in Western Europe. –

   Britain still has the <u>*highest teenage pregnancy rate in Western Europe*</u>.

3. Britain's teenage pregnancy rate is high despite the country being one of the world's biggest users of contraceptives. –

Although Britain is ___*one of the world's biggest users of contraceptives, the teenage*___
___*pregnancy rate is still high.*___

4. In the USA, thirty per cent of teenage girls who drop out of high school do so because they are pregnant. –

Pregnancy is the reason why ___*thirty percent of teenage girls drop out of high school in the*___.
___*USA.*___

5. Last year, teenage mothers in Britain gave birth to over 48,000 babies. –

48,000 babies were ___*born to teenage mothers in Britain last year*___.

6. Most teenage pregnancies are not planned. –

Only a few ___*teenage pregnancies are planned*___.

7. Teenage mums find it very difficult to continue with their education. –

Continuing with their education is not ___*easy for teenage mums*___.

LG3 The earth is still moving 🔍 📦

Complete the text with a correct form of the word given next to the text.

At 3.30 am on Wednesday 25 August, a magnitude 6.2 earthquake hit a region 100 km
north-east of Rome in Italy. The ___*most badly*___ (1) affected place

was Amatrice, a ___*beautiful*___ (2) medieval town where many

Italian people ___*were staying*___ (3) at the time to celebrate a local

festival. Firefighters and rescue teams worked ___*bravely*___

(4) for hours looking for ___*survivors*___ (5) in the rubble

of the collapsed buildings. However, among all the tragedy, there were some

___*stories*___ (6) of hope. For example, when rescue

___*workers*___ (7) pulled a 10-year-old girl from the ruins of a

___*building*___ (8). She had been trapped for 17 hours but was still

alive. Overall, the number of people who ___*were killed*___ (9) in the

region was more than 240.

bad
beauty
stay
brave
survive
story
work
build
kill

L1 Short dialogues

L 2.6 S 10

You will hear four short dialogues. There is <u>one</u> question for each dialogue. Decide which picture is the right answer to the question.

a) What is Tom's job?

✔

b) What is Katie doing in the summer holidays?

✔

c) At what time is their flight tomorrow?

✔

d) How are they going to get to Paris?

✔

L2 Going on a safari

You will hear a Kruger National Park tour guide talking about a safari the next day.
Complete the notes with the missing information.

 L 2.7 **S** 11

Kruger National Park Safari

Be at the meeting point at ___5:30___. Each car will take ___five___

people.

Take ___hats___ for protection.

You can get free ___(bottled) water___ from the drivers.

You might see animals like ___elephants/lions/rhinos/buffaloes/leopards (choose two)___.

At the rest camp you can buy ___lunch___.

You will be back at ___8___.

Don't forget your ___camera___.

L3 Radio ads

Read the statements. Then listen to three radio ads.
Which statement matches which ad? There are more statements than you need.
Write the letter of the statement next to the ad.
You can listen to the recording twice.

L 2.8 **S** 12

A This advert tells you how important it is to read stories to small children.
B This advert asks you to drive carefully on country roads.
C This advert warns drivers against listening to the radio in the car.
D This advert asks people to do something against climate change.
E This advert asks drivers to concentrate even if they know the route very well.
F This advert tells hikers that woods and nice countryside parks can be dangerous.

radio ad	statement
1.	D
2.	E
3.	B

L4 Children at work

L 2.9 S 13

**You will hear a radio programme with an interview about child labour.
Listen carefully and circle the right ending of the sentence.**

1. Liam and Bernie are from

   the Netherlands.

   (Ireland.)

   Denmark.

   England.

2. Bernie got interested in the 'Stop Child Labour'

   campaign because

   she worked for UNICEF.

   (her uncle talked to her about the problem.)

   she did a web project at school.

   she saw a TV programme about it.

3. Liam was

   (not really interested in the topic at first.)

   told about child labour in his football team.

   trying to get Bernie interested in the problem.

   a UNICEF volunteer in Pakistan.

4. Liam's new football

   was really expensive.

   cost over €30.

   was a present from Bernie.

   (was probably made by children in Pakistan.)

5. As a normal consumer you

   don't have the power to end child labour.

   (should try not to buy products made by children.)

   should not buy any imported products.

   can't get enough information.

6. On the website of the campaign you can

   get free toys.

   buy Fairtrade chocolate.

   (find out about typical child labour products.)

   chat to others about the problem.

7. Liam says that teenagers should

   stop eating chocolate.

   (inform other people about child labour.)

   buy more expensive things.

   give money to children in poor countries.

8. Liam and Bernie think that

   (all children should have the right and the time to

   go to school.)

   it's wrong for children to have after-school jobs.

   more children in Western Europe should work after

   school.

   most children have problems with full-time

   education.

L5 Different lives after school

a) Listen to three people and complete the grid with the information asked for.
Do not write sentences. Make notes or use keywords.

L 2.10 S 14

name	Will	Lisa	Anna
Where are they from?	New Zealand	Reading, England	Frankfurt, Germany
How old are they now?	21	19	23
What are they training or studying for at the moment?	degree in science and biology	training to become a doctor	training to be a vet
What did they do after finishing school and for how long?	qualified as a personal trainer, worked as a fitness instructor	went to Ghana for 11 months, taught English and science	went to England, worked on a farm in Devon for four weeks
What did they learn in that period?	more confident, focused and disciplined	learned about a different society and realized the importance of healthcare and clean water	learned to speak better English, found out what it was like living close to nature and working long hours in an international team

b) Which statement summarizes the attitude of which person?
Write the right name next to it. There are more statements than you need.

1. If you are really sure about what you want in life,
   you shouldn't waste time but go and do it.

   _Anna_____

2. If you don't enjoy studying hard at school,
   you shouldn't really go to university.

   _____

3. Working and living in a completely different culture
   can teach you what is really important in life.

   _Lisa_____

4. Taking time out to work hard in a real job can make
   you a better student.

   _Will_____

5. There is nothing better than being close to nature
   and animals if you want to focus again after finishing school.

   _____

R1 Signs and notices 👓

Look at the sign or notice in each task. Tick (✓) the statement that matches the correct meaning.

A

> Please switch off all mobile devices or gadgets before you enter the hospital rooms. They disturb our sensitive equipment and put lives in danger. Thank you!

  ☐ Sensitive electronic gadgets don't work in there.

  ☐ It's dangerous to enter these rooms.

  ✓ You must turn off your mobile or tablet before you go in.

  ☐ You shouldn't disturb anybody in the hospital rooms.

B

*Friday night's 7 pm English conversation course is cancelled due to illness.
Please contact Michelle (017263516) for new date and time.
Call evenings only.*

  ✓ The English course won't take place on Friday night.

  ☐ You must call Michelle when you are ill and can't go.

  ☐ You can call Michelle at any time.

  ☐ The new time for the course is 7 pm.

C

Sweaters from sweatshops? No, thank you!
Find out more about how to fight child labour worldwide.
Get active and come to our information evening. Friday, 6 pm, library.
Please register with Marc if you want to join as we only have 30 seats.

  ☐ If you want to buy new sweaters, you should go there.

  ☐ This is an invitation for an information evening about the new library.

  ✓ If you want to go to this, you should tell Marc first.

  ☐ You should bring your own chair because they have only 30 seats.

D

*Sitting your final exams and still no plan?
Our job counsellors will help you to find the right option for your future.
Just make an appointment NOW – online (careersadvice.co.uk) or
phone (0172 453789) – and your future might be more certain.*

  ☐ You can get help with your exam preparation here.

  ✓ People will discuss with you what you can do after school.

  ☐ You can sign up for service in the army here if you have completed your exams.

  ☐ Somebody will tell you the future on the phone.

R2 **Some crazy Facebook stories** 👓

Read the texts.

1
Colin Gunn, one of Britain's most dangerous gangsters, has been using Facebook to threaten his enemies from a high-security prison. From prison he was able to contact his over 560 'Facebook friends' freely whenever he wanted. Although serving a 35-year prison sentence, it is thought that he was still running a crime and drug empire from his cell with the help of Facebook. Gunn was allowed to open a Facebook account two months ago. The authorities have now closed it.

2
A family from Missouri was more than surprised when they found out that their picture ended up on a big poster advert for a supermarket in the Czech Republic. Mrs Smith had posted a photo, which showed her, her husband and her two children, on several social networking sites. Some weeks later a college friend of hers was driving through Prague and couldn't believe it when she saw the Smith family smiling from giant poster adverts of a supermarket. The store management said they had found the photo on the Web and thought it had been computer-generated. They apologized to the Smiths and took the posters down.

3
Craig Lynch, 28, who escaped from Hollesley Bay Prison, Suffolk, in September, was arrested by the Metropolitan Police in Kent yesterday with the help of Facebook.
Lynch, who has to spend seven years in prison for burglary, had set up a fan page on the social networking site after his successful escape, where he was posting comments and reports about his life on the run. More than 40,000 people all around the world were following his escape before his profile on Facebook was closed down. In the end his comments and updates on the networking site helped the police to find and arrest him.

4
Emma B., a 35-year-old woman from Lancashire, England, was shocked to find out about the end of her marriage on Facebook. Her husband Neil had posted a message on the social networking site which read: "Neil has ended his marriage to Emma." The woman said she had had no idea that her six-year marriage was over. She only found out when her friend from Denmark, who had read the message on Facebook, phoned her and wanted to check if she was all right.

a) Match the texts with the headlines. Fill in the number of the text.
There are more headlines than you need.

Headline	Number of text
Caught by Facebook	3
A modern end to a relationship	4
How to become an advert star without knowing	2
Find the right partner through Facebook	
Organised crime with the help of Facebook	1
Facebook helps to escape	

b) **Decide whether the following statements are true or false and tick (✓) the correct answer. Then finish the sentences. You can quote from the texts.**

1. Colin Gunn used his Facebook account for more than a year.

   This statement is

   ☐ true

   ✓ false

   because the text says __that Gunn was allowed to open the account two months ago__.

2. Mrs Smith found out about the photo from a friend who saw it.

   This statement is

   ✓ true

   ☐ false

   because the text says __a college friend couldn't believe it when she saw the Smith family__.

3. You can still see the Smiths' poster in Prague.

   This statement is

   ☐ true

   ✓ false

   because the text says __that the company apologized and took the posters down__.

4. Over 40,000 people helped the police to catch Craig Lynch.

   This statement is

   ☐ true

   ✓ false

   because the text says __40,000 people followed his escape__.

5. Emma B. was very surprised about her husband's message.

   This statement is

   ✓ true

   ☐ false

   because the text says __Emma was shocked__.

6. Emma and Neil had been married for almost a year.

   This statement is

   ☐ true

   ✓ false

   because the text says __Emma had no idea her six-year marriage was over__.

c) Finish the sentences using information from the texts.

1. Colin Gunn has to serve ___*a 35-year prison sentence*___ .

2. In the photo posted by Mrs Smith, you could see ___*her, her husband and her two children*___ .

3. Craig Lynch ran away from ___*Hollesley Bay Prison in Suffolk*___ .

4. On Facebook, Craig Lynch was posting ___*comments and reports about his life on the run*___ .

5. Emma was told about Neil's Facebook message when a friend called her from ___*Denmark to check if she was alright.*___

d) You are preparing an article about social networking sites for your school magazine. Now you have the chance to interview Emma B. **or** Mrs Smith about their experience. Ask them **four** questions. Use **four** different question forms.

Lösungsbeispiel: *1. What did you think when your friend told you about the picture?*

(Emma B.)   *2. Why do you think your husband posted the news on social media?*

3. Were you very sad?

3. What shocked you the most?

R3   What to do in South Africa?

These people are visiting South Africa and would love to do some interesting activities there. Read their profiles. Then read carefully about the activities. Find two suitable activities for each person/family and write the letters next to them. You can use each activity more than once.

The people	Activity 1	Activity 2
Paul (27) is a fitness instructor and wants to do something active and physically challenging, but he is not a big fan of one-off kicks like bungee jumping. He hates museums and would like to get out into the countryside.	B	G
The Macintyres have two children aged 9 and 13. They would like to stay in or around Cape Town and do something together as a family. They all love sports and other forms of physical activity.	F	C
Stella (21) is writing a project paper on apartheid and needs to find out more. She prefers to do her own thing rather than be taken round in a group on a guided tour. She also wants to stay active and would love to try out some new sports activity. As South Africa gets very hot, some water sports would be great. But she doesn't find looking at fish too exciting.	D	E
Ruth (42) is on a trip with her husband **John** (56). They would both love to meet some real South African people and learn more about South Africa's past. Ruth is physically active and adventurous but John isn't. However, he's a big sports fan and loves modern architecture. They want to go to places together.	A	H

The Activities

A Moses Mabhida Stadium

This spectacular modern structure was built for the FIFA World Cup in 2010. Beautiful white arches rise 100 metres into the air over the city of Durban. Your journey starts with a comfortable two-minute SkyCar ride up the arch, before you step onto a platform and take in the 360° views of Durban, the ocean and beyond. You can also enjoy a guided tour of the stadium. But that is not all. If you are brave enough, you can take a leap on the Big Rush Big Swing, the highest swing in the world. You swing out in a massive 220m arc and experience a safe (!) free fall of over 80 metres into the stadium bowl. Unforgettable!

B Cage Diving South Africa

Ever wanted to get up close and personal with a shark? Then try out some cage diving near the Cape Town coast. A great activity for adults of any age. After short safety instructions, you board one of our boats and we will take you to prime shark territory. Wet suits and weight belts are provided. Then you can climb into the cage – but you won't be completely under water yet. When you hear our experienced shark spotters shout "Down", you take a deep breath and hold yourself under water to watch the sharks in safety.

C The Springbok Experience

Rugby is one of South Africa's most popular sports, and now Cape Town is home to a world-class rugby museum – The Springbok Experience. Here you can find a well-designed exhibition that offers an excellent balance between informative and interactive experiences. There are touch screen games, alongside memorabilia of famous players. Particularly popular with children is the game zone where visitors can test their own rugby skills.

D Blyde Canyon Adventure

If you want to get your adrenalin pumping, then visit the Blyde Canyon Adventure Centre and tackle some whitewater rafting. Blyde River Canyon is Africa's second largest canyon and famous for its amazing scenery. The rafting is fast and furious and lets you test your skills and nerve along 8 km of white water.
Qualified guides will accompany you in their own rafts. As long as you are fit and healthy, no prior experience is necessary. The trip is not suitable for children or the elderly.

E Nelson Mandela's home

House 8115, Vilakazi Street, Orlando, Soweto, has become one of the most famous addresses in South Africa. It is where former South African President Nelson Mandela lived for more than 14 years. Now this house has become one of South Africa's most significant heritage sites because it tells the tale of the Mandela family in sound and film and gives an insight into the apartheid era. You can walk around the small house in your own time and experience their everyday life with the help of pictures and stories.

F The Yellowwood hiking trail

The trail at Kirstenbosch is a good choice for a hot summer's day hike. It is also suitable for children because it is manageable within a couple of hours. You can extend it into a whole morning as there are some great pools for a refreshing swim along the way. You will get a good view of Cape Town and you will see massive trees, too. In total, the trail is about 3 km. There is a little bit of steep climbing, but for the experienced hiker looking for exercise this might be too easy.

G Devil's Peak

Devil's Peak lies to the north-east of Table Mountain. The physically challenging path zigzags up to Saddle Rock. The route then continues to the 1,001m-high summit of Devil's Peak, where you will be rewarded with spectacular views of Cape Town. This is a more adult hike for the adventurous at heart and is best done in reasonable fitness and health. Approximately 4-5 hours.

H **Soweto and Apartheid Museum tour**
This 8-hour tour takes you on a journey to see the history of apartheid. After a guided tour of the Apartheid Museum, you will feel as if you had lived in the townships in the 1970s and 1980s, marching and protesting, or carrying the body of an injured friend into a nearby house. This powerful museum has become one of Johannesburg's most important tourist attractions. During the day-long tour, you will also meet local residents and have the chance to talk to them while enjoying lunch together.

R4 Children of another world 👓

Read the article.

Tomorrow morning in Haiti, some children will wake up to cook food they will never eat and wash clothes they will never wear. They will fetch food from the market and water from the well, all for a family that isn't theirs and that will probably never treat them as one of their own. Their names are Nadine, aged 9, or Fernande, aged 7, or Doudane, aged 14. They are just three out of more than 300,000 such children in Haiti today. They are "restaveks".   5

In the Creole language, "restavek" means "to stay or live with" somebody. But for the children who are called "restavek", that definition is incomplete. For them, it often means living with abuse, hunger, humiliation and without love.

"Restavek" is a form of modern-day slavery that has existed as part of Haitian culture for centuries. It affects about one in every 15 children. Two thirds of "restavek" children are girls. Typically   10
born into poor village families, "restavek" children are often given to relatives but also to complete strangers. Their families send them away in the hope of giving them a better life than the one they could have had at home.

Ideally, the children can go to school and are treated like one of the family. But often this is not the case. Instead, in their new homes they live like domestic slaves. For many children, the day is filled   15
with hard labour. Even the youngest ones have to carry heavy buckets of water, wash clothes with their hands and work unpaid in the fields – often for 14 hours a day. Usually their work ends when they are 15 because that is the age when a person must be paid for their work according to Haitian law. But by then, most of these children haven't learned to read or write and have nowhere to go.

Although not celebrated or positively accepted, the "restavek" system is generally tolerated by so-   20
ciety in Haiti. However, by international standards, it meets all the criteria of modern-day slavery.

Over the years different organizations like Restavek Freedom have given voices to "restavek" children. They try to raise international awareness to end this modern-day form of slavery but they also work in local communities in Haiti. For example, they send out child advocates to help mistreated "restavek" children. Here is one of their stories: 25

A Restavek Freedom Child Advocate found Jean-Daniel in 2009 when he was around 8 years old. His mother had died long before, and so his aunt came to get him and his older brother. Since then, he had been living in "restavek". He had to stay at home to complete chores while the other kids in his household went to school, and he didn't know how to read or write. He had no bed to sleep in at night, only the floor, and playtime was something he didn't know. With the help of the advocate,   30
he was able to start school. Jean-Daniel has been learning and making friends. He is also receiving better treatment at home. This year, his advocate proudly shared with us that he is at the top of his class! He has developed more self-confidence and he has something he didn't have before: hope.

It truly is amazing what having an advocate can do for a child living in "restavek"!

35

a) What is the general intention of the article? Circle the right statement.

The article was written

to tell the reader more about Haitian history.

to tell the reader about a special form of child labour in Haiti.

to ask the reader for help in funding an organization called Restavek Freedom.

to make "restavek" children think and break free from their situation.

b) Answer the following questions in your own words and in complete sentences. ⇨ **L p. 131**

1. How many children live in "restavek" in Haiti today?

_____

2. Why do their families send them into "restavek"?

_____

3. What are typical chores "restavek" children have to do? Give at least two examples.

_____

4. When and why does the "restavek" system usually end for a child?

_____

c) Match the correct sentence parts. There is one more ending than you need.

1. Although internationally "restavek" is seen as a modern form of slavery,
2. "Restavek" children should be sent to school by their host families,
3. There are some organizations
4. Host families often don't treat "restavek" children very well,
5. There are more girls than boys

A that are trying to help these children and get the world to see their situation.
B it has been tolerated as part of Haitian culture for a long time.
C for example by not giving them proper beds or enough food.
D but it means "to stay or live with" in Creole.
E but most of them never learn to read and write.
F who have to live in "restavek".

1. **B**   2. **E**   3. **A**   4. **C**   5. **F**

d) Read the last part of the text again and circle the right ending of the sentence.

1. Jean-Daniel

now works as a child advocate for Restavek Freedom.

lost his mother when he was around eight.

lived with his aunt and her family after his mother had died.

has no brothers or sisters.

2. In the household he came to live in   none of the children could go to school.

all children were treated the same.

he was able to play with children his age.

(he didn't have a proper place to sleep.)

3. With the help of Restavek Freedom,   he has become a child advocate.

he left the family he stayed with.

he has met and helped other "restavek" children.

(he has become a very good student at school.)

W1 Working as an au pair ✏

You would like to work as an au pair in an English-speaking country.
Fill in this form with your personal information.   *Lösungsbeispiel:*

Name: __Heike Sandau__   Sex: ☐ male   ✔ female

Nationality: __German__

Country you would like to work in: __England__

Date you would like to start working: __20 August__

What age range would you like to au-pair for? __4 to 9 years old__

What childcare experience have you had? __I often babysit my younger brother__

What would you be willing to do to help with the housework? __I am happy to do the hoovering, empty the dishwasher and do laundry, however I would rather not clean the bathroom.__

What are your hobbies? __I enjoy cooking, singing and swimming. I also go running every morning.__

W2 My weekend ✏️

Choose one of the pictures and imagine you took it last weekend.
   Write a text/comment for a blog or your social media.
   Explain the picture and what it has to do with
   how you spent your weekend.

A

C

B

Lösungsbeispiel: (Picture A)

Hey guys!

So I guess you're wondering what the picture is all about.

That's me, in the middle, with my friends, as we cook. Basically, I decided to have a pizza party for my friends last weekend!

Everyone brought their favourite toppings and I provided the basic ingredients, like tomato and cheese. We had a competition with different prizes. We had a prize for the best tasting pizza, and the one which looked the tastiest — I won that! Of course, that had nothing to do with my mum being the judge …

How was everyone else's weekend?

Lösungsbeispiele: (Pictures B und C) ⇨ L p. 131

W3 Spending a year abroad ✎

You want to spend a year abroad after finishing school. Choose <u>one</u> of the following adverts and write an email or letter to apply for the job. Don't forget to write why you would be a good candidate/why you would like to do the job, what experience you have and when you could start work.

We are looking for a

German-speaking au pair

We live in the English countryside, one hour's drive from London. Our children are four and seven years old.

You should be responsible and tidy and have some experience with children. You will take the children to school, look after them in the afternoons and do a little housework like shopping or cooking.

Free food and accommodation, an English course and pocket money are part of this offer.

Apply to **Mr and Mrs Sheen**
26 Church Street
Cambridge CB23 2SG
England

HELP IN BUSY YOUTH HOSTEL NEEDED

Are you able to speak English and another foreign language?
Can you work with a computer?
Do you enjoy talking to people?
Then you are perfect for us. Enjoy some time in Sydney, Australia and earn money at the same time.

Applications to **Glebe Village Backpackers**, Fred Simmonds, 256 Glebe Point Road, Glebe NSW 2037, Australia OR
<u>Fred@GlebeBackpackers.com</u>

ARE YOU GOOD AT WORKING WITH YOUR HANDS AND DON'T MIND A LITTLE DIRT?

Do you like animals and are not afraid of them?
Are you interested in working with nature and wildlife?
Durrell Wildlife Park on the Channel Island of Jersey (between France and England) needs helpers and animal carers.
No experience necessary. We just need your enthusiasm.

Write to Durrell Wildlife Park, Ms Kathrin Boons, Les Augrés Manor, La Profonde Rue, Trinity, Jersey, Channel Islands, JE3 5BP

Lösungsbeispiel: (au pair)

Dear Mr and Mrs Sheen,

I am writing to apply for the position of au pair after seeing your advert online.

My name is Lena Böll and I live in Hamburg, Germany. I would love to work in England, look after your children and learn English at the same time.

As you will see from my CV, I have experience working with children because I babysit regularly and last summer I worked as a nanny for a German family. At home I am expected to do the housework and the cooking regularly because both of my parents

work late.

My school year finishes at the end of June so I would be able to start at the beginning

of July.

I look forward to hearing from you soon.

Yours sincerely,

Lena Böll

Lösungsbeispiel: (Glebe Village Backpackers)

Dear Mr Simmonds,

I am writing to you to apply to help at your youth hostel.

My name is Lena Böll and I am from Germany. At the end of this month I will finish school

and I am planning to travel around the world. I would like to go to Australia but

unfortunately, I don't have enough money to do all the things I want to do. So it would be

ideal if I could travel and work at the same time to earn some money.

I think my English is good enough. I love talking to other people, especially if it means I

can practise my English. I work well with others and I am good with computers, too.

I look forward to hearing from you.

Yours sincerely,

Lena Böll

Lösungsbeispiel: (Durrell Wildlife Park) ⇨ L p. 131

MD1 Healthy holidays

Your family is planning a trip to South Africa. Your mum has found the following tips on the Internet and wants you to tell her in German what they are about. Write down five important tips in German.

> **Planning a trip to South Africa? Here are some tips for staying healthy.**
>
> Before you travel, check with your doctor which medication (e.g. anti-malaria drugs) or vaccinations (e.g. tetanus) you need.
> Many diseases are caused by insect bites. So when you are there, make sure
> - you have anti-insect spray and use it.
> - you wear long-sleeved shirts, long trousers and hats outdoors.
> - you stay indoors in the evening and at night.
> - you sleep in beds that are covered with nets or other insect protection if you are not in an air-conditioned room.
>
> Also don't touch or feed any animals and drink only bottled water.
> You should only eat food that is completely cooked.

⇨ **L p. 132**

_____

_____

_____

_____

_____

MD2 Notices

You are at the school club with your English exchange partner. You find the following notices on the noticeboard.

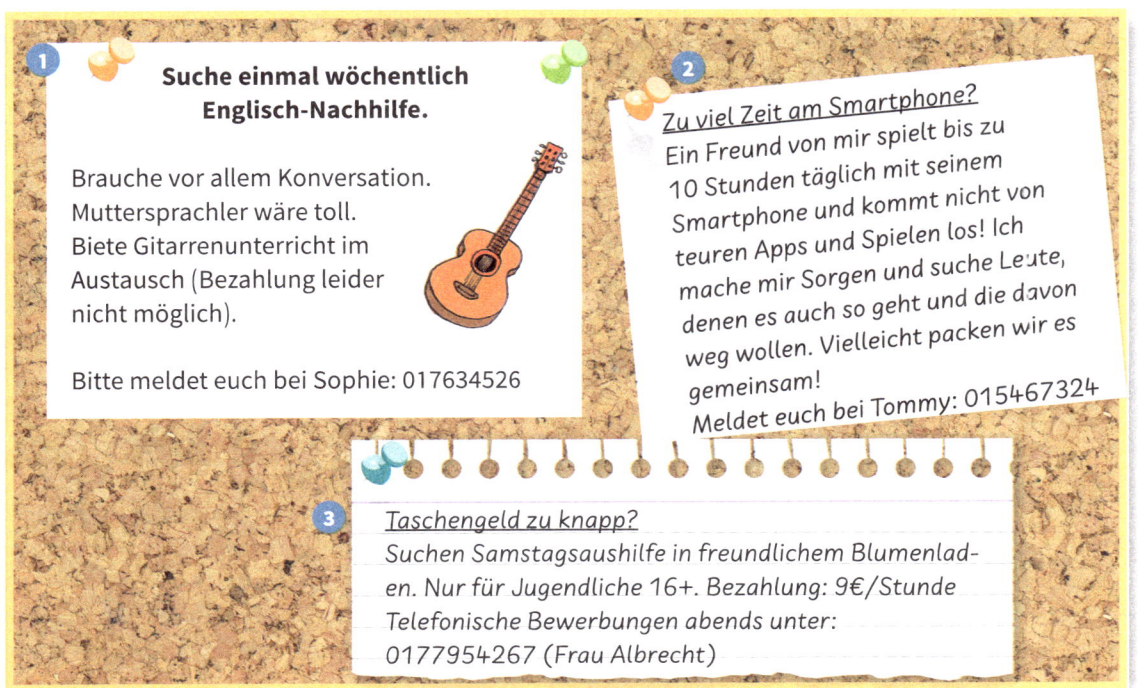

1

Suche einmal wöchentlich Englisch-Nachhilfe.

Brauche vor allem Konversation.
Muttersprachler wäre toll.
Biete Gitarrenunterricht im
Austausch (Bezahlung leider
nicht möglich).

Bitte meldet euch bei Sophie: 017634526

2

Zu viel Zeit am Smartphone?
Ein Freund von mir spielt bis zu
10 Stunden täglich mit seinem
Smartphone und kommt nicht von
teuren Apps und Spielen los! Ich
mache mir Sorgen und suche Leute,
denen es auch so geht und die davon
weg wollen. Vielleicht packen wir es
gemeinsam!
Meldet euch bei Tommy: 015467324

3

Taschengeld zu knapp?
Suchen Samstagsaushilfe in freundlichem Blumenlad-
en. Nur für Jugendliche 16+. Bezahlung: 9€/Stunde
Telefonische Bewerbungen abends unter:
0177954267 (Frau Albrecht)

Tell your exchange partner in English what the notices are about. Write down at least two details for each notice.

⇨ L p. 132

_____

_____

_____

_____

_____

_____

_____

MD3 New media stars 🇬🇧

You are part of an exchange visit to England. You are asked to write a text for the English school magazine about new media stars for young Germans.
Read about the two German YouTube stars and choose <u>one</u> of them to write your text about. Just give the main facts about the person and his/her career. Do not translate word for word.

Der offizielle Name von **Dagi Bee** ist so kompliziert, dass sie ihn bestimmt schon deshalb geändert hat. Im Personalausweis der 1994 geborenen Düsseldorferin steht Dagmara Nicole Ochmanczyk. Als Dagmara machte sie Fachabitur und wurde Industriekauffrau, als Dagi Bee ist sie ein YouTube-Star. Der YouTuber und Rapper LionT, mit dem sie von 2011 bis 2015 zusammen war, brachte Dagi Bee zur Musik. Bei einigen seiner Songs war sie dabei. Aber das Dabeisein reichte ihr bald nicht mehr, und schon im Oktober 2012 veröffentlichte sie ihr erstes eigenes Video, ‚NO-GOs bei Jungs!'. Ein witziges Video über das, was Jungs tun sollten, um bei ihren Freundinnen anzukommen. Immer mehr Videos mit Kosmetik- und Modetipps folgten. Dagi Bees YouTube-Kanal hat inzwischen zweieinhalb Millionen Abonnenten und 430 Millionen Aufrufe. Und die hübsche Blondine mit der Vorliebe für Nagellack genießt Star-Kultstatus. Videos wie ‚Schönheitswahn – sich selber lieben lernen' und ‚Probleme unter Geschwistern', Schminktipps zu Halloween, der ‚No-Make-up-Look' und Challenges unterschiedlichster Art stellt Dagi Bee seitdem ins Netz, zeigt ihren Fans auch schon mal peinliche Selfies und natürlich die Musikvideos, die sie mit KC Rebell und anderen aufgenommen hat. Sie gehört zu den Top 20 der erfolgreichsten deutschen YouTube-Kanäle. Immer wieder tritt Dagi Bee auch live auf und sorgt für einen Massenauflauf. Im Fernsehen und in Kinofilmen wie _Fack ju Göhte 2_ oder _Er ist wieder da_ konnte man sie ebenfalls sehen.

Dner ist ein Multitalent in sozialen Netzwerken. Seit 2011 erreicht er über YouTube, Instagram und Twitter ein Millionenpublikum. Er ist einer der erfolgreichsten und populärsten deutschen Internetstars. Zurzeit ist er mit über 2,7 Millionen Abonnenten auf Platz 11 der meistabonnierten Kanäle Deutschlands. Die wenigsten dürften ihn bisher unter seinem richtigen Namen Felix von der Laden kennen. Er nennt sich selbst Dner, und er ist einer der größten YouTube-Stars Deutschlands. Geboren wurde er 1994 in Reinbek bei Hamburg und begann nach dem Abitur ein Studium der Medienwissenschaften in Köln, das er jedoch abbrach, als seine YouTube-Aktivitäten immer mehr Zeit in Anspruch nahmen. Dner ist vor allem für seine Let's Plays – also das Vorspielen und gleichzeitige Kommentieren von Games – zu _Minecraft_ und _Grand Theft Auto V_ bekannt. Im Gegensatz zu anderen Let's Playern, die häufig viele unterschiedliche und aktuelle Games spielen, konzentriert sich Dner vorwiegend auf diese beiden Spiele. Daneben veröffentlicht er auch immer wieder Clips von seinen Erlebnissen in der realen Welt, zum Beispiel von einer Longboard-Tour quer durch Deutschland.

Aber Dner verdient auf der Videoplattform nicht nur mit seinem Haupt-Channel Geld. Mittlerweile tritt er auch regelmäßig in auf *Coke TV* veröffentlichten Videos auf. Das Spannende an der Sache: Dner zeigt, dass Youtuber die Werbestars der Stunde sind und dass immer mehr große Firmen auf diese jungen Internet-Promis setzen.

Lösungsbeispiel: (Dagi Bee)

'Dagi Bee' is a successful YouTube star who gives fashion advice and makes music videos.

Dagi Bee is actually called Dagmara Nicole Ochmanczyk and she first started working as

a saleswoman. Her boyfriend LionT was a rapper and YouTuber and she appeared in some

of his songs. In October 2012, Dagi Bee made her first YouTube video on her own and

today her channel is watched by millions of people.

Dagi Bee is now so popular that she has even been on TV and in films.

Lösungsbeispiel: (Dner) ⇨ **L p. 132**

LG1 What's your network? 🔍 📚

Read the text and fill the gaps with one or two suitable words.

Many teens today (1) __*use*__ social networking sites as their main form

(2) __*of*__ communication.

Facebook, WhatsApp, Instagram and all the others don't only give teenagers the chance of (3)

__*staying*__ in touch. Social networking sites are definitely the virtual communities

of the 21st (4) __*century*__.

One of the (5) __*most*__ famous communities is Facebook. It was founded

(6) __*by*__ the Harvard student Mark Zuckerberg in 2004 and in the beginning

it was only there to help new Harvard students to get to know (7) __*each other*__.

Since then, the number of registered Facebook users (8) __*has risen*__ to almost 2

billion people worldwide. That makes Facebook one of the (9) __*largest*__ social

networking sites, (10) __*although*__ there are others that compete for a share of the

market.

LG2 Different networks 🔍 📦

Read the text and choose the correct word or expression for each space from the grid below. Fill in the correct letter.

Twitter was started (1) __B__ 2006. It is a very popular instant messaging system that lets a (2) __C__ send short text messages to a list of followers. It was designed to keep friends and colleagues informed every day. Twitter messages are (3) __D__ "tweets" and usually people can send or receive them via mobile phone or the Internet. These messages are (4) __A__ to 140 characters. Recently this messaging service (5) __B__ an instrument for international political leaders to inform the public about their opinions and policies (6) __A__ without using the press.

Especially (7) __B__ with teenagers today are image-sharing mobile applications (8) __C__ Snapchat or Instagram. Snapchat (9) __A__ in 2011 as an image messaging application (10) __D__ focused on the idea of living in the moment because the images you can share there are only temporary and self-deleting. That seems to appeal to younger people. Over 50 per cent of Snapchat users are aged (11) __C__ 16 and 24.

	A	B	C	D
1	at	in	of	for
2	people	somebody	person	individual
3	named	formed	known	called
4	limited	ruled	short	allowed
5	was	has become	is used	functions
6	directly	direct	personal	honest
7	lovely	popular	favourite	most
8	example	how	like	meaning
9	started	has started	was starting	starts
10	what	who	it	that
11	from	at	between	with

1R The present tense

a) The simple present
- Das *simple present* verwendest du, um über …
    Gewohnheiten und regelmäßige Handlungen,
    aufeinander folgende Handlungen zu sprechen,
    Zustände, die längere Zeit andauern zu sprechen.
- Die Verneinung bildest du mit **don't**, bei *he, she* und
    it mit **doesn't**. Bei der Verneinung von Sätzen mit
    be, **can** oder **have got** brauchst du **don't** oder
    doesn't nicht.
- Entscheidungsfragen sind Fragen, auf die man mit
    „Ja" oder „Nein" antworten kann.

b) The present progressive
- Das *present progressive* verwendest du, wenn du
    sagen möchtest, was jemand gerade tut oder was
    gerade passiert – also für Vorgänge, die gerade
    ablaufen und noch nicht abgeschlossen sind.
- So bildest du das *present progressive*
    Form von **be (am, is, are)** + **Infinitiv des Verbs** +
    Endung **-ing**.
    *He **is drinking** orange juice.*
- Für die Verneinung fügst du einfach ein **not** hinter
    die Form von *be* ein:
    *Caroline is **not** writing a letter.*
- Entscheidungsfragen und Kurzantworten bildest du
    so:
    Is George **helping** his mum? – **Yes, he is.**
    Are Sam and Zoe **playing** tennis? – **No, they
    aren't.**
- Bei Fragen mit Fragewort stellst du das Fragewort an
    den Satzanfang: ***What are** you **doing**?*

2R The present perfect

a) The present perfect
- Das *present perfect* verwendest du,
    … wenn etwas irgendwann, noch nie oder noch
    nicht geschehen ist:
    *Holly **has** never **tried** peanut butter.*
    … wenn ein Vorgang in der Vergangenheit noch
    Auswirkungen auf die Gegenwart hat:
    *David **has cleaned** the kitchen.* (sie ist noch
    sauber).
- Du bildest es mit **have / has** + **Partizip Perfekt**.
    *I **have watched** a film.*
- Die Verneinung bildest du mit **haven't / hasn't** +
    Partizip Perfekt.
    *She **hasn't learned** English*
- Entscheidungsfragen im *present perfect* bildest du,
    indem du das Subjekt und **have/has**
    vertauschst. Bei Fragen mit Fragewörtern steht das
    Fragewort am Satzanfang.

b) The present perfect progressive
- Das *present perfect progressive* verwendest du, um
    über Handlungen oder Ereignisse zu sprechen,
    die in der Vergangenheit begonnen haben und
    bis in die Gegenwart andauern. Dabei ist die
    Handlung oder das Ereignis selbst wichtiger als der
    Zeitpunkt, zu dem sie stattgefunden haben.
- So bildest du das *present perfect progressive*:
    **Form von *have* + *been* + *-ing*-Form des
    jeweiligen Verbs**
    *The girl **has been crying** for hours.*

c) The present perfect with since and for
- **Since** und **for** werden häufig mit dem *present perfect*
    verwendet. Wenn du von einem genauen Zeitpunkt,
    an dem eine Handlung oder ein Ereignis begonnen
    hat, sprechen möchtest, benutzt du **since**, z. B. **since**
    2011, **since** *Monday,* **since** *then.*
    *Kian has written four covering letters **since** Friday.*
- Wenn du aber einen Zeitraum angibst (Tage, Monate,
    Jahre usw.), benutzt du das *present perfect* mit **for**,
    z. B. **for** *six months,* **for** *a long time.*
    *Jessica has repaired cars **for** more than five years.*

3R The past tense

a) The simple past
- Das *simple past* verwendest du, wenn du über etwas
    sprechen willst, das in der Vergangenheit liegt und
    abgeschlossen ist – z. B. eine Geschichte oder ein
    Erfahrungsbericht.
- So bildest du das *simple past*: Endung **-ed** an den
    Infinitiv anhängen: **watch + ed** ➜ **watched**
- Bei unregelmäßigen Verben wird das *simple past* nicht
    mit *-ed* gebildet. Die unregelmäßigen Formen must
    du lernen.
- Die Verneinung bildest du bei den meisten Verben
    mit **didn't (did not)**. Das Verb selbst bleibt im
    Infinitiv, weil **didn't** schon die Vergangenheit
    anzeigt.
    Bei **was/were** bildest du die Verneinung mit **not**.
- Entscheidungsfragen und Kurzantworten bildest du
    mit **did/didn't**, bei **was/were** mit **not**.
    Did you **go** on holiday? – **Yes, I did.**
    Was it good? – **No, it wasn't.**

b) The past progressive
- Das *past progressive* drückt aus, …
    was jemand gerade tat oder was gerade passierte.
    was gerade vor sich ging, als etwas anderes
    geschah.
- So bildest du das *past progressive*:
    Simple past-Form von **be (was/were)** + **Infinitiv des
    Verbs** + Endung **-ing**
    *The girl **was wearing** her pajamas.*
- Für die Verneinung fügst du einfach ein **not** hinter
    die Form von *be* ein:
    *The band was**n't** playing all the time.*

• Fragen und Kurzantworten bildest du so:
Was the boy **listening** to music? – **Yes, he was.**
What was the band **playing**?

4R The past perfect

Das *past perfect* verwendest du, wenn du über eine Handlung sprechen möchtest, die vor einer anderen Handlung in der Vergangenheit stattgefunden hat. Die zweite Handlung steht im *simple past*. Beide Handlungen sind abgeschlossen.
• So bildest du das *past perfect* : **had** + **Partizip Perfekt (past participle)**

1. Handlung: *past perfect*	2. Handlung: *simple past*
Because people **had found** out about her Catholic boyfriend,	Sadie lost her job.
After Sadie **had lost** her job,	she started working for Mr Blake.

• Die Verneinung bildest du mit **hadn't** + **Partizip Perfekt** *(past participle)*.
Because their families **hadn't allowed** *them to see each other, Kevin and Sadie kept their love a secret.*
• Wenn du das *past perfect* bildest, musst du auf das Partizip Perfekt achten (➔ LiF 2R).

5R The past perfect progressive

Das *past perfect progressive* verwendest du, um über Handlungen oder Ereignisse zu sprechen, die vor einem bestimmten Zeitpunkt in der Vergangenheit bereits begonnen hatten und über den Zeitpunkt hinaus andauerten. Dabei ist die Handlung oder das Ereignis und deren Dauer wichtiger als der Zeitpunkt, zu dem sie stattgefunden hatten.
• So bildest du das *past perfect progressive*: **had** + **been** + **-ing-Form des jeweiligen Verbs**
The girl **had been reading** for hours when her father asked her to stop.
• Die Verneinung bildest du mit **hadn't**.
Because they **hadn't been earning** much money, they could only afford a small room in London.
• Fragen und Kurzantworten bildest du so:
Had Kevin **been working** for long? – **Yes, he had.**
How had they **been travelling**?

6R The future tense

a) Die Zukunft mit *will* (The *will*-future)
Wenn du über die Zukunft sprechen willst, benutzt du das *will-future*. Mit dem *will-future* kannst du Vermutungen aussprechen und Vorhersagen oder Versprechen äußern.
• Das *will-future* bildest du mit **will** und dem **Infinitiv des Verbs**. Auch **will** hat eine Kurzform. Sie lautet **'ll**. **Will** ist in allen Personen gleich.
I **will help** you.
You**'ll find** new friends.
The weather **will be** great tomorrow.
• Die Verneinung bildest du mit **will not** oder der Kurzform **won't**.
He **won't get** a dog.
• Fragen und Antworten bildest du so:
Will Tom **get** a job? – **Yes, he had.**
Where **will** you **live** in ten years? – I think I **will** live in Berlin.

b) Die Zukunft mit *going to* (The *going to*-future)
Die Zukunft mit *going to* verwendest du, wenn du sagen willst, was jemand für die Zukunft plant oder vorhat. Im Deutschen gibt es keine Zeitform, die dem *going to* entspricht. Du hast aber verschiedene Möglichkeiten, es wiederzugeben:

We**'re going to** fly to London tomorrow.	*Wir werden morgen nach London fliegen. Wir möchten/wollen morgen nach London fliegen. Wir planen/haben vor, morgen nach London zu fliegen.*

• Du bildest die Zukunft mit *going to* mit einer **Form von be** + **going to** + **Infinitiv des Verbs**.
*I***'m going to fly** *to Sydney next week.*
Rajiv **is going to help** *his parents in their shop.*
• Die Verneinung bildest du mit **not**.
I**'m not going to call** her tomorrow.
• Fragen und Antworten bildest du so:
Are you **going to watch** the film? – **No, I'm not.**
What **are** you **going to do**? – I**'m going to call** Dan.

7R The future progressive

Das *future progressive* verwendest du, …
• um Dinge zu beschreiben, die zu einem bestimmten Zeitpunkt in der Zukunft ablaufen werden.
Tomorrow at 3 o'clock I **will be flying** to London.
• um über gewohnheitsmäßige Handlungen oder Vorgänge in der Zukunft zu sprechen.
When I come home from school, my brother **will be waiting** for me.

• Du bildest das *future progressive* mit **will** + **be** + **-ing-Form des jeweiligen Verbs**.
I'll be visiting my aunt in Cape Town on Tuesday.
Darren will be seeing his cousins next week.

8 The future perfect

Das *future perfect* verwendest du, um Handlungen zu beschreiben, die zu einem bestimmten Zeitpunkt in der Zukunft abgeschlossen sein werden.
Darren will have been in South Africa for three weeks next Saturday.
• Du bildest das *future perfect* mit **will** + **have** + **Partizip Perfekt (*past participle*)**.
By this time next year I'll have finished school.
The students will have learned a lot when they leave school.

9R Modal verbs and their substitute forms

Die meisten Modalverben haben nur Formen für das *simple present*.
Im *present perfect, simple past* und im *will-future* verwendest du deshalb die Ersatzformen.
a) Fähigkeit: *can/can't – be able to/not be able to*
• Mit **can** kannst du sagen, …
  was jemand tun kann
  was jemand tun darf.
• Die Ersatzform von *can* ist **be able to**. Im *simple past* kannst du aber auch **could** benutzen.
  *Emma and Charlie **were able to** help Mr Miller.*
  *Rajiv **couldn't** do his maths homework because it was too difficult.*
b) Erlaubnis: *can/can't – be allowed to/not be allowed to – must not*
• ***Can/can't, be allowed to*** und ***must not*** benutzt du, wenn du …
  um etwas bittest
  um Erlaubnis fragst oder jemandem etwas erlaubst
  etwas verbietest.
• ***Must not*** oder die Kurzform ***mustn't*** klingt wie im Deutschen „muss nicht", heißt aber „etwas nicht dürfen".
c) Notwendigkeit: *must/have to – needn't/don't have to*
• ***Must*** klingt wie das deutsche Wort „muss" und heißt auch *müssen*.
  In der Regel kannst du **must** auch durch **have to/has to** ersetzen.
• ***Must*** hat keine eigene Vergangenheitsform.
  Daher wird die *simple past*-Form von **have to** benutzt.
• Wenn du sagen willst, was jemand nicht tun muss, benutzt du **don't/doesn't have to**.

• Auch mit ***need not*** oder ***needn't*** kannst du ausdrücken, dass etwas nicht notwendig ist.
d) Empfehlung: *should/shouldn't*
• Mit ***should*** drückst du aus, dass etwas deiner Ansicht nach passieren sollte:
  *You **should** leave now if you want to catch the bus.*
• Mit ***should*** kannst du auch die Meinung einer anderen Person erfragen.
  *Which T-shirt **should** I buy?*

10R Conditional clauses, type I

Ein Bedingungssatz besteht aus einem *if*-Satz *(if-clause)* und einem Hauptsatz *(main clause)*:
• Der *if*-Satz nennt eine Bedingung. Der Hauptsatz drückt aus, was passiert, wenn die Bedingung erfüllt ist.
• Im *if*-Satz steht das *simple present*, im Hauptsatz das *will-future*.
  If you **miss** the bus, you **will be** late.
• Bedingungssätze können entweder mit dem *if*-Satz oder mit dem Hauptsatz beginnen. Wenn sie mit dem *if*-Satz beginnen, werden sie mit einem Komma getrennt.
  If you go to the cinema, I'll come with you.
  I'll come with you if you go to the cinema.
• Im Hauptsatz kannst du auch Modalverben (z. B. *can, should*) oder den Imperativ verwenden.
  *If it snows, we **can go** inside.*
  *If you like her, you **should call** her.*
  *If you need help, **ask** Lisa.*

11R Conditional clauses, type II

• Mit dem Bedingungssatz, Typ II, drückst du aus, was unter einer nur gedachten Bedingung passieren würde oder könnte. Dabei geht es um Ereignisse, die <u>unwahrscheinlich</u> oder <u>unmöglich</u> sind.
• Der *if*-Satz *(if-clause)* steht im *simple past*. Im Hauptsatz *(main clause)* steht **would** oder **could** vor dem Infinitiv.
  If I **went** to South Africa, I **would visit** Robben Island.
  If Mike **had** a chance to go to Hermanus, he **would go** whale watching.
• Bei *if*-Sätzen heißt es üblicherweise *"if I were …"*, aber du kannst auch *"If I was …"* sagen. Beide Formen sind hier richtig.
  *If I **were** really good at football, I would be famous.*
  *If I **was** rich, I would be happy.*

12R Conditional clauses, type III

- Mit dem Bedingungssatz, Typ III, drückst du aus, was in der Vergangenheit hätte passieren können, aber nicht passiert ist. Die Bedingung im *if*-Satz ist <u>nicht mehr erfüllbar</u>.
- Der *if*-Satz *(if-clause)* steht im *past perfect*.
  Im Hauptsatz *(main clause)* steht **would** oder **could + have** + **Partizip Perfekt** *(past participle)*:
  If the Internet **hadn't been invented**, people **would have found** other ways to communicate.
  If there **hadn't been** any social networks,
  Dara **would have gone** out more often to see her friends in town.

13R The gerund

Wird ein Verb wie ein Nomen verwendet, nennt man das Gerundium *(gerund)*. Im Englischen hängst du dafür ein *-ing* an den Infinitiv des Verbs:
Going *to school by bike can be fun.*
- Das Gerundium kann Subjekt eines Satzes sein.
  Buying fair trade products is good for the workers.
- Das Gerundium folgt oft nach bestimmten Verben wie *like*, *love*, *enjoy*, *hate*, *start* und *stop*.
  He **likes meeting** new people.
- Du benutzt das Gerundium auch nach bestimmten Ausdrücken wie *can't stand*, *be good at*, *be bad at*, *be afraid of*, *be fond of* oder *look forward to*.
  I'm **fond of travelling**.
  She **can't stand swimming**.

14 The passive

Wenn mit einer Person, einem Tier oder einer Sache etwas getan wird, kannst du das durch das Passiv ausdrücken. Man benutzt es dann, wenn nicht wichtig oder nicht klar ist, wer handelt oder gehandelt hat.
Today people write most letters on a computer. – Today most letters **are written** *on a computer.*
- Das Passiv bildest du so:
  Form von *be (am/is/are/was/were/will be/has been/have been/had been)* + Partizip Perfekt *(past participle)*
  Oklahoma **was hit** by a tornado.
  Emergency shelters **have been set** up.
- Wenn du in einem Passivsatz doch einmal die handelnde Person oder die Ursache für etwas nennen willst, hängst du sie mit *by* („von", „durch") an den Satz an:
  Emergency shelters have been set up **by** *the Red Cross.*

15 Modal verbs with passive forms

Du kannst Modalverben und ihre Ersatzformen wie *can, should, need to, have to* usw. in Kombination mit dem Passiv verwenden. Damit drückst du aus, dass eine Handlung ausgeführt bzw. nicht ausgeführt werden soll, muss, kann usw.
- Das Passiv mit Modalverben bildest du so:
  can/could/must/should/ *… + be + Partizip Perfekt (past participle)*
  Covering letters **must be written** on a computer.
  Interviews **can be done** over the phone, too.
  You **should be prepared** to answer the employer's questions.

16R Word order and questions

a) Aussagesätze
- Der Bauplan für englische Aussagesätze sieht so aus:

(Vorfeld)	Subjekt	Häufigkeits-adverb	Verb	Objekt	andere Ergänzungen
Last week	Karim		was		ill.
	Amy	usually	eats	two apples	for lunch.

- Häufigkeitsadverbien *(adverbs of frequency)* stehen meist zwischen Subjekt und Verb. Häufigkeitsadverbien stehen allerdings immer hinter den Formen von *can* und *be*.
  We can **sometimes** *get up late on Saturdays.*
  She's **always** *late.*
- Orts- und Zeitangaben stehen in der Regel am Ende des Satzes. Dabei steht immer "Ort" vor "Zeit".
  My aunt lived in Cape Town from 2001 to 2016.
  Um eine Zeitangabe stärker zu betonen, kannst du sie auch an den Satzanfang stellen:
  In 2015 we went to visit my aunt in South Africa.

b) Fragen
- Ja/Nein-Fragen bildet man so:

Hilfsverb	Subjekt	Verb	andere Ergänzungen
Is	Torge	talking	on the phone?
Does	Emma	know	the answer?

- Fragen mit Fragewort *(where/ what/when/who/why/ what/how)* folgen demselben Bauplan, aber sie beginnen mit dem Fragewort.
  Where is Jessica?
- Bei Fragen mit *who* braucht man kein *do* oder *does*, wenn *who* Subjekt ist:
  Who *celebrates Diwali?*

17R Verb + object + infinitive with to

- Nach bestimmten Verben, die eine Erlaubnis, einen Wunsch oder einen Willen ausdrücken (**advise, ask, allow, tell, want/would like**), kannst du den Infinitiv mit **to** verwenden. **To** steht in diesen Fällen nach dem Objekt.
  John's dad **tells** his son **to** be more careful on the Internet.
- Bei der Verneinung wird ein **not** vor **to** gestellt.
  Mrs Collins **asked** her daughter **not to** spend too much time online.

18R Relative clauses

a) Relativpronomen (Relative pronouns)
Mit Relativsätzen kannst du eine Person oder eine Sache genauer beschreiben.
- Ein Relativsatz beginnt meist mit einem Relativpronomen: **who, which** oder **that**. Dabei verwendest du **who** für Personen und **which** für Dinge.
  People **who** are married usually live together.
  Many people are in a relationship **which** is happy.
- Das Relativpronomen **that** kannst du sowohl für Dinge als auch für Personen benutzen.
  The promises **that** couples make when they get married are often broken.
  There are lots of people **that** think a relationship should end in a marriage.

b) Relativsätze ohne Relativpronomen (Contact clauses)
Das Relativpronomen (*who, which, that*) kann im Englischen weggelassen werden, wenn es das Objekt des Relativsatzes ist. Wenn dem Relativpronomen ein **Verb** folgt, muss das Relativpronomen bleiben. Folgt ein **Substantiv**, kannst du das Relativpronomen weglassen. Im Deutschen ist dies nicht möglich.
People **who are** in love are mostly happy.
Problems **which can** be found in any relationship must be solved together.
The time **(which) people** spend together is really important.

c) Partizipien zur Verkürzung von Relativsätzen (Participles used to shorten relative clauses)
Im Englischen gibt es zwei Partizipien: das *present participle*, das auf -ing endet, und das *past participle* (= 3. Verbform), das bei regelmäßigen Verben auf -ed endet. Die unregelmäßigen Formen findest du auf den Seiten 333 – 335. Diese Partizipformen kannst du benutzen, um einen Relativsatz zu verkürzen. Dabei ersetzt …
- das *present participle* eine Form im Aktiv und
- das *past participle* eine Form im Passiv.

		Relativsatz	
Beispiel im Aktiv	Teenagers	**who want to** get married	must talk to their parents.
	Teenagers	**wanting to** get married	must talk to their parents.
Beispiel im Passiv	Some of the things	**that are said** in an argument	can hurt.
	Some of the things	**said** in an argument	can hurt.

19 Defining and non-defining relative clauses

Um eine Person oder eine Sache genauer zu beschreiben, verwendest du Relativsätze *(relative clauses)*. Es gibt zwei Arten von Relativsätzen: notwendige Relativsätze *(defining relative clauses)* und nicht notwendige Relativsätze *(non-defining relative clauses)*.
- Die **notwendigen Relativsätze** beginnen in der Regel mit einem Relativpronomen *(relative pronoun)* und bestimmen das Wort näher, auf das sie sich beziehen (→ LiF 16R). Sie können nicht weggelassen werden – der Hauptsatz ergibt sonst keinen Sinn:
  Zola is one of the "kwaito" artists who are listened to most.
  Cape Town is a city that I have always wanted to visit.
- **Nicht notwendige Relativsätze** liefern zusätzliche Informationen über eine Person oder Sache im Hauptsatz. Sie können weggelassen werden, da der Hauptsatz auch ohne sie verständlich bleibt. Nicht notwendige Relativsätze sind vom Hauptsatz durch Kommas getrennt.
  This is my friend Isabel, who is working as a volunteer animal carer in South Africa. –
  Das ist meine Freundin Isabel, die …
  The books, which I bought yesterday, are about Nelson Mandela's life. – Die Bücher, die …, behandeln Nelson Mandelas Leben.
- Das Relativpronomen **that** wird im nicht notwendigen Relativsatz nicht verwendet.
  Es kann nur im notwendigen Relativsatz stehen.
  The songs that I listened to were about life in the townships.

20 Participles used to shorten adverbial clauses

- Neben dem *present* und dem *past participle* gibt es im Englischen auch noch das *perfect participle*. Dieses verwendest du, um Adverbialsätze zu verkürzen.
- Das *perfect participle* bildest du so:
  having + **Partizip Perfekt *(past participle)***

	verkürzter Adverbial-satz
After **he had finished** school, Tom wanted to live abroad for some time.	**Having finished** school, Tom wanted to live abroad for some time.
Because **they wrote** many covering letters, the teenagers found a job quickly.	**Having written** many covering letters, the teenagers found a job quickly.

21R Reported speech

- Wenn du berichten willst, was jemand gesagt hat, verwendest du die indirekte Rede *(reported speech)*.

Direkte Rede		**Indirekte Rede**	
		Begleitsatz	Wiedergegebene Aussage
Juno: "I'm bored"	➔	*Juno says (that)*	*she is bored.*

- Die indirekte Rede besteht aus einem Begleitsatz und der wiedergegebenen Aussage. Beide Satzteile können durch *that* verbunden werden, man kann es aber auch weglassen.
- Wenn du etwas berichten willst, das du gerade gehört hast und das jetzt noch stimmt oder allgemeingültig ist, benutzt du im Begleitsatz und in der wiedergegebenen Aussage die Zeitform der Gegenwart.
  Dave: "Smoking is unhealthy." ➔ Dave **thinks** *(that) smoking is unhealthy.*
- Im Allgemeinen stehen die Verben im Begleitsatz und in der wiedergegebenen Aussage in der Vergangenheit. Die Zeitform der wiedergegebenen Rede rückt dann sozusagen eine Stufe weiter in die Vergangenheit als die direkte Rede (Zeitverschiebung = *backshift of tenses*).
- Meistens musst du Teile der indirekten Rede anpassen oder ergänzen, damit dein Gesprächspartner versteht, was du meinst. Das betrifft zum Beispiel die Pronomen und die Verbform, aber auch Angaben zu Ort und Zeit.
- Wenn du eine Frage wiedergeben möchtest, die jemand anders gestellt hat, benutzt du *if* oder *whether*. Auch bei Fragen musst du darauf achten, dass die Zeitformen sich ändern.
  *Doctor: "Do you **have** any questions, Juno?"* ➔ *The doctor asked Juno **if** she **had** any questions.*
- Wenn die Frage mit einem Fragewort eingeleitet wird, übernimmst du einfach das Fragewort:
  *Juno's mum: "**How old is** Paulie?"* ➔ *Juno's mum wanted to know **how old** Paulie **was**.*

22R Linking words

Linking words sind Wörter, mit denen du Sätze verbinden kannst.
- Mit den Konjunktionen **and**, **but**, **so** und **or** verbindest du Hauptsätze.
  Sadie is Protestant **and** Kevin is Catholic.
  They had to be careful **or** they would be in danger.
- Mit Konjunktionen wie z. B. **before**, **because**, **although**, **if**, **when** und **while** verbindest du einen Hauptsatz mit einem Nebensatz.
  Kevin was badly injured **because** Brian and his friends beat him up.
  Mr Blake saw Kevin **while** he was walking his dog in the park.
- Du kannst deinen Satz auch mit dem Nebensatz beginnen. Dann steht die Konjunktion am Anfang.
  Although Brede knew that Sadie loved Kevin, she asked her to leave him.

23R Comparison of adjectives

Wenn du Personen oder Sachen miteinander vergleichen möchtest, kannst du ein Adjektiv steigern. Die Steigerungsformen heißen ***comparative*** (Komparativ) und ***superlative*** (Superlativ).
a) Steigerung von Adjektiven mit *-er* und *-est*
- Einsilbige Adjektive (z. B. *cheap, old, young*) werden durch das Anhängen von **-er** und **-est** gesteigert.
  cheap – cheap**er** – (the) cheap**est**
- Bei zweisilbigen Adjektiven, die auf **-y** enden, wird aus dem *-y* ein **-i**.
  pretty – prett**ier** – (the) prett**iest**
- Einige Adjektive haben unregelmäßige Steigerungsformen. Diese Formen musst du wie Vokabeln lernen.
b) Steigerung von Adjektiven mit *more* und *most*
- Mehrsilbige Adjektive werden mit **more** und **most** gesteigert. Du stellst dabei **more** oder **most** vor das Adjektiv. Das Adjektiv bleibt unverändert.
  interesting – **more** interesting – (the) **most** interesting
c) Vergleichssätze
- Willst du ungleiche Dinge miteinander vergleichen, benutzt du den Komparativ mit ***than***.
  Vegetables are **healthier than** meat.

- Sind die Eigenschaften von zwei Dingen oder Personen gleich, benutzt du *as ... as*.
Table Mountain is **as interesting as** the Kruger National Park.

24R Adverbs of manner

Wenn du beschreiben möchtest, wie jemand etwas tut oder wie etwas geschieht, benutzt du ein Adverb der Art und Weise. Adverbien der Art und Weise bildest du, indem du an das Adjektiv die Endung *-ly* anhängst.

Adjektiv	Adverb
loud	loud**ly**
bad	bad**ly**
slow	slow**ly**

- Bei manchen Adverbien ändert sich die Schreibweise, wenn *-ly* angehängt wird: *-y* wird zu *-ily*; *-le* wird zu *-ly*; *-l* wird zu *-lly*.

Adjektiv	Adverb
happy	happ**ily**
easy	eas**ily**
terrible	terrib**ly**
beautiful	beautiful**ly**

- Einige Adverbien haben Sonderformen, die du wie Vokabeln lernen musst. Manche Adjektive und Adverbien sind gleich.

Adjektiv	Adverb
good	**well**
fast	**fast**
hard	**hard**

- Adverbien der Art und Weise stehen nach dem Verb. In Sätzen mit Objekt stehen sie nach dem Objekt.
Mira works **hard**.
Ali talks to the journalist **secretly**.

25R Comparison of adverbs

Du weißt bereits, wie Adjektive gesteigert werden (➔ LiF 23R).
Für die Steigerung von Adverbien gelten die gleichen Regeln.

*Amy cooks **more deliciously** than Jason.*
Amy kocht leckerer als Jason.
*Kathy works **harder** than other managers.*
Kathy arbeitet härter als andere Manager.
- Einsilbige Adverbien werden durch das Anhängen von *-er* und *-est* gesteigert.
fast – fast**er** – (the) fast**est**
- Mehrsilbige Adverbien, die auf *-ly* enden, steigerst du mit **more** und **most**.
slowly – **more** slowly – (the) **most** slowly
- Es gibt auch unregelmäßige Steigerungsformen, die du wie Vokabeln lernen musst.
well – **better** – (the) **best**

26 Sentence adverbs

- Beziehen Adverbien wie **luckily**, **before**, **while**, **finally**, **after**, **however**, **moreover** oder **unfortunately** sich nicht nur auf ein einzelnes Verb, sondern auf einen gesamten Satz, sind es so genannte Satzadverbien.
Unfortunately, Darren was feeling a little sick.
Jessica learns a lot at the restaurant. **Moreover**, she meets very interesting people.
I would like to go to the cinema. **However**, I have to do my homework first.
Finally, they saw the whales in Hermanus.
Luckily, she reached the car **before** the tiger could get her.

27 Inversion

- Im Englischen steht das Subjekt in Haupt- und auch in Nebensätzen normalerweise immer vor dem Verb/Hilfsverb (be, do, have, ...) (➔ LiF 16R). In manchen Fällen steht aber das Hilfsverb vor dem Subjekt.
- Insbesondere nach negativen oder einschränkenden Adverbien wie **not only ... but also**, **no sooner ... than**, **hardly**, **only after**, **only when**, **at no time**, **so ... that**, **never ... that** liegt im Englischen eine Inversion vor, also eine Umkehrung der üblichen Reihenfolge des Hilfsverbs und des Subjektes. Die Reihenfolge ist dann z. B. so: **Form von *do* + Subjekt + Infinitiv des Verbs**
New Orleans <u>lies</u> north of the Gulf of Mexico and is surrounded by the Mississippi River and Lake Pontchartrain. ➔ **Not only** <u>does</u> New Orleans <u>lie</u> north of the Gulf of Mexico, **but** it is **also** surrounded by the Mississippi River and Lake Pontchartrain.
She <u>did not know</u> that this day would change her life. ➔ **Hardly** <u>did</u> she <u>know</u> that this day would change her life.

28R Prop words

- Du benutzt **one**, um ein Nomen nicht zu wiederholen.
  *I have two brothers. The little **one** is five and the other **one** is seven years old.*
  Ich habe zwei Brüder. Der kleine ist fünf und der andere ist sieben Jahre alt.
- Wenn das Bezugswort im Plural steht, musst du **ones** benutzen.
  *Raúl cleans shoes, mostly expensive **ones** from business people.*
  Raúl putzt Schuhe, meistens teure von Geschäftsleuten.
- Im Deutschen kannst du das Nomen einfach weglassen, wenn du es nicht wiederholen möchtest. Im Englischen ist das nicht möglich. Du musst die Stützwörter **one** oder **ones** benutzen.
  *Which T-shirt should I take? The yellow **one** or the blue **one**?*
  Welches T-Shirt soll ich nehmen? Das gelbe oder das blaue?

29 Emphatic *do*

- Das *emphatic do* benutzt du, um einer Aussage besonderen Nachdruck zu verleihen. Wenn du betonen möchtest, dass etwas *wirklich* wahr ist oder *wirklich* stattgefunden hat, kannst du *do*, *does* oder *did* + **den Infinitiv des jeweiligen Verbs** zur Betonung verwenden.
  *I **did** do my homework.*
  *I **do** have to admit that it's not always easy.*
  *I **do** like you.*
  *I enjoy it, but I **do** feel exhausted at times.*
- Du kannst das *emphatic do* nicht mit *be* verwenden

30 Have sth done, make sb do sth

- **Have sth done** verwendest du, um auszudrücken, dass eine Person/ein Unternehmen/… etwas von jemand anderem ausführen lässt.
  *Companies **have** their products **imported** from China.*
  – Unternehmen lassen ihre Produkte aus China importieren.
- Du verwendest den Ausdruck so:
  Subjekt + Form von *have* + <u>Objekt</u> + Partizip Perfekt *(past participle)*
  Manufacturers **have** <u>their jeans</u> **produced** in Asia.
  They **have had** <u>the cotton for their clothes</u> **bought** in India since 1988.
  Clothes companies **are having** <u>their products</u> **sold** all over the world.

- **Make sb do sth** verwendest du, um auszudrücken, dass eine Person/ein Unternehmen/… (aktiv) jemanden veranlasst/dazu bringt, etwas zu tun.
  *Fairtrade organizations **make** workers **use** less dangerous chemicals. –*
  Fairtrade-Organisationen bringen die Arbeiter dazu, weniger gefährliche Chemikalien zu verwenden.
- Du verwendest den Ausdruck so:
  Subjekt + Form von *make* + <u>Objekt</u> + Infinitiv des jeweiligen Verbs
  The factory owner **makes** <u>the girls</u> **work** for little money.
  International companies **have made** <u>manufacturers</u> **produce** cheap clothes.

Vergleiche deine Antworten mit den Lösungen und zähle deine Punkte.
Rechne deine Gesamtpunktzahl aus und lies dann die Auswertung und die
Lerntipps unten auf der Seite.

TEST YOURSELF
LÖSUNGEN **1**

1 Listening: Needing help

Meine Punkte:

a) She is worried that she might be pregnant.
b) 1 she is worried someone will find out; 2 can buy a home pregnancy test anywhere; 3 she will have a lot of options if she's pregnant; 4 take the test with her best friend

Für jede richtige Lösung erhältst du zwei Punkte.

von 10

2 Writing: YOUR plan

Beispiellösung:
Ten years from now I think I'll work as a joiner and I'll study to become an architect. I want to be an architect but I want to learn a job first so that's what I'll do. I'll live with my younger brother and we'll have a cool flat in the centre of town. We'll have a lot of parties and there will always be friends over. I hope we'll have a clean flat. I'm sure we'll share the household duties. My brother is good at cooking and I'm good at cleaning so it will be fair. I won't have children. Maybe I'll have children in 15 years but first I have to finish my studies.

Prüfe, ob
– du zu den vorgegebenen Punkten Informationen geben und weitere Themen (z. B. Tiere, Geschichte) ergänzt hast.
– sich dein Text flüssig liest (logischer Aufbau, verschiedene Satzkonstruktionen)
Für den Inhalt erhältst du bis zu 10 Punkte, für die sprachliche Richtigkeit bis zu 5 Punkte.

von 15

3 Reading: Home life

1 false, line 2; **2** false, line 7; **3** true, 10-11; **4** true, line 13; **5** false, line 17; **6** true, lines 17-18; **7** true, line 27; **8** not in the text

Für jede richtige Lösung erhältst du zwei Punkte.

von 16

4 Grammar: About 'Juno'

1 Mariah said that it was the best film she had ever seen. **2** Rick thought that Ellen Page was a talented actress. **3** Cynthia said that she had liked the songs best. **4** Nathalie said that the parents in the film were really helpful and understanding. **5** Brad said that young people who watched the film would think more about teenage pregnancy.

Für jede richtige Lösung erhältst du einen Punkt.

von 5

Auswertung

Meine Punkte insgesamt: **von 46**

46 – 33 Punkte: *Well done!* Du hast gleich zu Beginn des Schuljahres einiges dazugelernt. Bleib dran, dann machst du auch in Klasse 10 weiterhin gute Fortschritte!

32 – 23 Punkte: *Good job!* Du hast eine gute Leistung erbracht, aber du kannst dich noch steigern. Die Tipps unten helfen dir bei den Aufgaben, bei denen du Fehler gemacht hast.

22 Punkte und weniger: *Try harder!* Du merkst sicher selbst, dass deine Leistungen noch nicht ausreichen. Bei welchen Aufgaben hattest du die meisten Schwierigkeiten? Woran lag es? Die Tipps unten helfen dir beim Wiederholen und Üben. Streng dich an! Du kannst das schaffen.

Lerntipps:
- **Listening:** Lies die Aufgabe genau, bevor du den Text hörst. Dann weißt du schon ungefähr, was in dem Hörtext vorkommt. Nun brauchst du nur noch konzentriert zuzuhören. Du kannst den Hörtext auch mehrfach hören, um dein Hörverstehen zu trainieren.
- **Writing:** Sammle zunächst Ideen und mache dir Notizen. Auf der *How to write*-Seite im *Textbook* findest du eine Schritt-für-Schritt Anleitung zum Schreiben und Überarbeiten eigener Texte.
- **Reading:** Lies die *true*, *false* und *not in the text* Aussagen einzeln nacheinander und suche jeweils die entsprechenden Aussagen im Text. Vergleiche genau, dann kannst du leicht die Übereinstimmung oder die Unterschiede feststellen.
- **Grammar:** Wenn du Schwierigkeiten bei dieser Aufgabe hattest, lies die Erklärungen im LiF-Teil noch einmal und notiere dir einige Beispielsätze.

TEST YOURSELF LÖSUNGEN

Vergleiche deine Antworten mit den Lösungen und zähle deine Punkte. Rechne deine Gesamtpunktzahl aus und lies dann die Auswertung und die Lerntipps unten auf der Seite.

1 Listening: Linda

Meine Punkte:

a) Linda's plans for her future
b) **1** wrong; **2** right; **3** right; **4** right; **5** wrong; **6** right

Für jede richtige Lösung erhältst du zwei Punkte.

 von **14**

2 Reading: Unicef

1 The aims of the UN are to secure world peace and human rights. **2** The basic rights for children are the right to life, survival and development, the right to protection and the right to take part in cultural, family and social life. **3** Unicef was founded in 1946. **4** Unicef is mainly active in developing countries and areas of conflict. **5** Unicef supports countires with medical, financial and educational help.

Für jede richtige Lösung erhältst du zwei Punkte.

 von **10**

3 Writing: Your life after school

Beispiellösung:
When school is over I will go to the US. I will work as an au-pair for one year. I'm really looking forward to it. After the year I will travel through the US for about 3 months. I will go to New York City and and I will go to the Grand Canyon because I have always wanted to see that. When I come back to Germany I will start an apprenticeship as a kindergarten teacher. I like kids and I think the job will be fun. Later I'll have my own kids and maybe I'll be married.

Prüfe, ob
– du zu den vorgegebenen Punkten Informationen geben und weitere Themen ergänzt hast.
– sich dein Text flüssig liest (logischer Aufbau, verschiedene Satzkonstruktionen)
Für den Inhalt erhältst du bis zu 10 Punkte, für die sprachliche Richtigkeit bis zu 5 Punkte.

 von **15**

4 Grammar: At school

1 for; **2** since; **3** for; **4** since; **5** for; **6** since

Für jede richtige Lösung erhältst du einen Punkt.

 von **6**

5 Speaking: Different worlds

Beispiellösung:
In the first picture there are three girls playing video games. They're having fun and I think they're at the home of one of the girls. They're happy and laughing. The second picture shows a girl in a classroom. I think she's bored and maybe annoyed. In this picture I can see a girl and a few other children. They're carrying something heavy on their heads. I think they're somewhere where it's hot. They probably feel tired and exhausted. In the last picture there is also a girl who has to carry something on her head. It looks really difficult. She's somewhere hot and she's annoyed and tired.

Bei einem Kurzreferat ist es wichtig, dass du frei sprichst. Du solltest mit einer kurzen Beschreibung der Bilder beginnen. Für den Inhalt und für deine Vortragsweise erhältst du je 5 Punkte.

 von **10**

Auswertung

Meine Punkte insgesamt: von **55**

55 – 39 Punkte: Sehr gut! Du arbeitest hervorragend mit und erzielst gute Ergebnisse.
38 – 28 Punkte: Gut, aber du kannst mehr schaffen! Sieh dir an, welche Aufgaben dir schwer gefallen sind, und nutze die Lerntipps, um dich zu verbessern.
27 Punkte und weniger: Schade, das war noch nicht ganz so gut. Nutze die Lerntipps, um gezielt zu üben, dann geht's schnell aufwärts!

Lerntipps:
- **Listening:** Versuche beim ersten Hören herauszufinden, worum es in dem Dialog ganz allgemein geht. Dann lies die Aussagen genau durch, um zu entscheiden ob sie falsch oder richtig sind.
- **Reading:** Lies den Text eventuell merhmals, um die Antworten zu finden.
- **Writing:** Falls Dir nicht gleich etwas einfällt, mache erst einmal ein paar Notizen.
- **Grammar:** Du kannst dir Grammatik-Regeln besser merken, wenn du sie jemandem erklärst, zum Beispiel deinen Geschwistern oder einem Freund.
- **Speaking:** Sieh dir die Bild genau an und mache dir Notizen zu den Fragen.

Vergleiche deine Antworten mit den Lösungen und zähle deine Punkte. Rechne deine Gesamtpunktzahl aus und lies dann die Auswertung und die Lerntipps unten auf der Seite.

TEST YOURSELF LÖSUNGEN **3**

1 Listening: Benjamin Kau

Meine Punkte:

a) 1965
b) 1 South Western Townships; **2** services; **3** protest against apartheid;
4 which lasted for days and hundreds of people were killed;
5 in a classroom for safety; **6** were not allowed to take part in the Olympics; **7** famous worldwide; **8** to vote; **9** president

Für jede richtige Lösung erhältst du zwei Punkte.

von **20**

2 Writing: Living under apartheid

Beispiellösung:
During apartheid, black people could not live where they wanted to. They were not allowed to marry whom they wanted or get the job they wanted. They had to live in certain places rather than where they wanted to. They could not be buried where they wanted to be buried when they died. They were not allowed to do these things because in the mind of the white-skinned people of South Africa, black people were not human beings and they were not South African.

Prüfe, ob
– du zu den vorgegebenen Punkten Informationen geben und weitere Themen ergänzt hast.
– sich dein Text flüssig liest (logischer Aufbau, verschiedene Satzkonstruktionen)
Für den Inhalt erhältst du bis zu 10 Punkte, für die sprachliche Richtigkeit bis zu 5 Punkte.

von **15**

3 Reading: The cradle of humankind

1 true, line 3 and 16; **2** not in the text; **3** true, 10-11; **4** true, line 7;
5 false, line 10; **6** true, line 15; **7** false, lines 18-19; **8** true, line 21

Für jede richtige Lösung erhältst du zwei Punkte.

von **16**

4 Words: Definitions

1 national park; **2** boarding pass; **3** prison; **4** aquarium; **5** sights;
6 apartheid

Für jede richtige Lösung erhältst du einen Punkt.

von **6**

5 Speaking: Going to South Africa

Beispiellösung:
I would love to go to South Africa. I would look at some of the cities, especially Cape Town. Cape Town has some amazing sights. I would love to see the Two Oceans Aquarium and I would love to go up Table Mountain. I would also visit Robben Island to find out what Nelson Mandela's life in prison was like. It would be amazing to go to the Kruger National Park as well. I would love to see animals like lions and giraffes in the wild.

Bei einem Kurzreferat ist es wichtig, dass du frei sprichst. Für den Inhalt und für deine Vortragsweise erhältst du je 5 Punkte.

von **10**

Auswertung

Meine Punkte insgesamt: von **67**

67 – 47 Punkte: Sehr gut! Du arbeitest hervorragend mit und erzielst gute Ergebnisse.
46 – 34 Punkte: Gut, aber du kannst mehr schaffen! Sieh dir an, welche Aufgaben dir schwer gefallen sind, und nutze die Lerntipps, um dich zu verbessern.
33 Punkte und weniger: Schade, das war noch nicht ganz so gut. Nutze die Lerntipps, um gezielt zu üben, dann geht's schnell aufwärts!

Lerntipps:
- **Listening:** Lies dir die *How to… listen*-Seite noch einmal genau durch und konzentrier dich auf den Hörtext.
- **Reading:** Unterstreiche wichtige Informationen im Text, so findest du sie zur Bearbeitung der Aufgabe schnell wieder.
- **Writing:** Das *Theme* gibt dir viele Information darüber was du schreiben könntest. Lies deinen Text genau und prüfe, ob du alle wichtigen Punkte aufgegriffen hast.
- **Words:** Schau dir die Texte im Theme und die Vokabellisten noch einmal genau an, falls ud hier Schwierigkeiten hattest.
- **Speaking:** Mache dir vorher Notizen und übe deinen Vortrag mehrmals.

4

TEST YOURSELF
LÖSUNGEN

Vergleiche deine Antworten mit den Lösungen und zähle deine Punkte. Rechne deine Gesamtpunktzahl aus und lies dann die Auswertung und die Lerntipps unten auf der Seite.

1 Listening: Tornado hunters

Meine Punkte:

a) They should be careful. They should do exactly as they are told when hearing a tornado warning.
b) 1 last year; **2** storm chaser tour; **3** comfortable car/ truck;
 4 weather measuring equipment; **5** storm spotters;
 6 dangerous or not; **7** safe distance

Für jede richtige Lösung erhältst du zwei Punkte.

von **16**

2 Writing: Being social

Beispiellösung:
I'm in touch with my friends every day. We normally message each other all the time. We send pictures and memes to each other. I sometimes send emails but normally I just write messages. It's quicker and you get a reply at once. I use a few social media sites like Facebook and Instagram. My favourite one is Snapchat at the moment. It's super easy to be in touch with everyone on there.

Prüfe, ob
– du zu den vorgegebenen Punkten Informationen geben und weitere Themen ergänzt hast.
– sich dein Text flüssig liest (logischer Aufbau, verschiedene Satzkonstruktionen)
Für den Inhalt erhältst du bis zu 10 Punkte, für die sprachliche Richtigkeit bis zu 5 Punkte.

von **15**

3 Reading: The tornado

1 8; **2** in the evening; **3** in the basement; **4** EF-4, the strongest type;
 5 about 90% of the town; **6** They could go to emergency shelters.

Für jede richtige Lösung erhältst du zwei Punkte.

von **12**

4 Words: Missing words

1 survive; **2** safe; **3** earthquakes; **4** smartphone; **5** tornado;
6 forecast; **7** communicate; **8** social network

Für jede richtige Lösung erhältst du einen Punkt.

von **8**

5 Speaking: The internet

Beispiellösung:
I don't think I could live without the Internet. It's one of the most important things in my life. I use it all the time to chat with friends, look up information, post pictures, watch videos and so on. Without the Internet I don't really know what I would do. I'd probably have to go and visit my friends or read a book. I would definitely have fewer friends.

Bei einem Gespräch ist es wichtig, dass du gut zuhörst und auf deinen Partner/deine Partnerin reagierst. Für ein gelunges, flüssiges und logisches Gespräch erhaltet ihr jeweils 10 Punkte.

von **10**

Auswertung

Meine Punkte insgesamt: von **61**

61 – 43 Punkte: Sehr gut! Du bist im Englischen schon sehr sicher. Weiter so!
42 – 31 Punkte: Du hast eine Menge gewusst, aber an einigen Stellen hakt es noch. Bleib weiterhin am Ball, dann
 kannst du dich schnell verbessern.
30 Punkte und weniger: Na ja, das war noch nicht ganz so gut. Aber du kannst dich verbessern. Du findest Vorschläge
 in den Lerntipps.

Lerntipps:
- **Listening:** Du kannst dir Filme auf Englisch ansehen um deine Ohren zu trainieren. Wenn du einen Film schaust, den du schon kennst, geht es richtig gut! Als Nächstes kannst du ja dann einen Film auf Englisch anschauen, den du noch nicht kennst.
- **Reading:** Je öfter du englische Texte liest, desto besser läuft's auch in der Schule. Lies doch mal einen Comic auf Englisch oder leih dir ein englisches Buch aus. Je mehr Englisch du liest, desto leichter fällt es dir.
- **Writing:** Schau dir noch einmal die How to write-Seite an und halte dich an die Tipps.
- **Speaking:** Die *wordbank* H bietet dir Hilfe für dieses Gespräch.

Liebe Schülerin, lieber Schüler,

Portfolio-Fragebögen wie in diesem Heft kennst du
schon aus dem letzten Schuljahr.

Bei Das bringe ich mit kannst du eintragen,
was du bisher im Englischunterricht gelernt hast.

Die Fragebögen jedes Mal aus,
wenn ihr ein Theme im Textbook und Workbook
komplett abgeschlossen habt.

Das geht so:
Sieh dir z. B. den Abschnitt Hören an.
Lies die Sätze und überlege, wie gut du das
kannst, was dort beschrieben ist.

Hinter den meisten Sätzen steht, wo du nachschlagen kannst,
wenn du nicht genau weißt, was gemeint ist.
Es kann auch sein, dass ihr im Unterricht nicht alle Übungen gemacht habt. Dann kannst du den
betreffenden Satz überspringen.

Hinter jedem Satz stehen drei Kästen.
Wenn du meinst, dass du etwas schon gut kannst, dann kreuze den Kasten **Kein Problem!** an.
Wenn du dich bei einer Aufgabe noch nicht sicher fühlst, dann kreuze
den Kasten **Das geht schon ganz gut** an.
Wenn du noch große Schwierigkeiten hast, kreuze **Das muss ich noch üben** an.

Wenn du den zweiten oder dritten Kasten angekreuzt hast, solltest du dir die angegebenen Aufgaben
im Textbook oder Workbook noch einmal gründlich ansehen und sie wiederholen.

Es ist nicht schlimm, wenn du nicht gleich alles kannst.
Im Laufe des Schuljahres gibt es viele Übungen und Aufgaben, mit deren Hilfe du die Sprache lernen
wirst. Wichtig ist, dass du dir klar machst, was du schon kannst und was du noch besser machen
musst.

Und jetzt: Viel Spaß!

Hören

Ich kann gezielt Informationen aus einem Dialog
heraushören. (TB 7, 8)
Ich kann Songs bestimmten Gefühlslagen zuordnen. (TB11)
Ich kann eine Geschichte verstehen, wenn ich sie mitlese.
(TB 12)

P Das bringe ich mit

Ich heiße: _____

Meine Schule heißt: _____

Ich lerne jetzt seit _____ Jahren Englisch.

Außerdem spreche ich folgende Sprachen:

_____

Ich fand den Englischunterricht bisher: _____

_____

_____

Das habe ich schon gelernt:

Ich kann …

☐ verstehen, was mir jemand erzählt.

☐ einen Dialog verstehen und sagen, worum es geht.

☐ ein Radio- oder Fernsehinterview hören und es verstehen.

☐ verstehen, worum es in einem Lesetext geht.

☐ unbekannte Wörter aus dem Zusammenhang erschließen.

☐ Lesetexten gezielt bestimmte Informationen entnehmen, z. B. um eine bestimmte Frage zu beantworten.

☐ mithilfe eines Beispieltextes oder von Fragen über Themen aus meinem Alltag schreiben.

☐ den Schluss einer Geschichte schreiben.

☐ Fotos, Cartoons und Bilder beschreiben.

☐ Rollenspiele zu verschiedenen Themen durchführen.

☐ über Dinge sprechen, die ich im Alltag mache.

Außer im Englischunterricht habe ich Englisch schon in folgenden Situationen gebraucht:

_____

Diese Themen haben mich in Camden Market am meisten interessiert:

_____

Ich habe ein Buch auf Englisch gelesen. Es heißt:_____

Dieses Buch würde ich gerne auf Englisch lesen: _____

Mein englisches Lieblingslied ist: _____

Im Englischunterricht konnte ich am besten:

    neue Texte beim Hören verstehen   eigene Texte schreiben

    neue Texte beim Lesen verstehen   etwas vortragen

    mich mündlich am Unterricht beteiligen   mit anderen zusammenarbeiten

_____

_____

Ich kann mit einem Wörterbuch arbeiten: ja   nein

Meine Tests und Klassenarbeiten waren:

  sehr gut   gut   ganz ordentlich   mal so – mal so   nicht so gut

Das möchte ich im neuen Schuljahr verbessern:

_____

_____

_____

	Kein Problem!	Das geht schon ganz gut.	Das muss ich noch üben.

Hören

Ich kann einem Dialog folgen und Informationen ordnen. (TB 5)

Ich kann einem Song das passende Bild zuordnen. (TB 9)

Ich kann Anrufe bei einem Beratungsdienst verstehen und Informationen heraushören. (WB 10)

Sprechen

Ich kann mich über einen längeren Text unterhalten. (TB 2, 3)

Ich kann Vermutungen über die Zukunft zweier Leute anstellen. (TB 7)

Ich kann Bilder beschreiben und Vermutungen dazu äußern. (TB 9)

Ich kann über das mögliche Ende eines Films sprechen. (TB 12)

Lesen

Ich kann Auszüge aus einem Roman verstehen. (TB 2, 3, 6, 7)

Ich kann einer Filmkritik Informationen entnehmen. (TB 10)

Schreiben

Ich kann eine Kurzbiografie schreiben. (WB 2)

Ich kann meine Gedanken zu einem Text, den ich gelesen habe, aufschreiben. (TB 6b)

Wortschatz

Ich kann Adjektive nach ihrer Bedeutung sortieren. (WB 3)

Ich kann mir unbekannte Wörter aus dem Kontext erschließen. (WB 9b)

LERN- UND ARBEITSTECHNIKEN

Ich kann im Textbook nachschlagen, um Informationen zu finden zu:

- Grammatikregeln (TB LiF ab S. 190)
- Wörtern aus Theme 1 (TB Words ab S. 215)
- Wortfeldern aus Theme 1 (TB Wordbanks ab S. 161)
- Lerntipps und Hilfen (TB Toolbox: How to … TB ab S. 172)

	Kein Problem!	Das geht schon ganz gut.	Das muss ich noch üben.

Hören

Ich kann mir zu einem Dialog über Zukunftspläne Notizen machen. (TB 4)

Ich kann einem Interview Informationen entnehmen. (TB 12)

Sprechen

Ich kann über meine Zukunftspläne Auskunft geben. (TB 2)

Ich kann mich über meine Pflichten im Haushalt unterhalten. (TB 10c)

Ich kann über Statistiken sprechen. (TB 11)

Lesen

Ich kann ein Gedicht lesen und interpretieren. (TB 1)

Ich kann E-Mails Informationen entnehmen. (TB 3)

Ich kann einen Zeitungsartikel über Kindarbeit so gut verstehen, dass ich Lückensätze dazu ergänzen kann. (TB 13)

Schreiben

Ich kann einen Text über meine Zukunftspläne schreiben. (WB 1)

Ich kann eine E-Mail beantworten. (TB 3c)

Wortschatz

Ich kenne Wörter aus dem Bereich *work*. (WB 3)

Ich kann Wörter in einem Wörterbuch nachschlagen. (WB 9)

LERN- UND ARBEITSTECHNIKEN

Ich kann mit anderen zusammenarbeiten und meine Ideen im Gruppengespräch erläutern. (TB 1b)

Ich kann eine *word web* erstellen. (TB 2)

Ich kann mir Notizen machen und diese mit einem Partner/einer Partnerin besprechen und vergleichen. (TB 4c)

	Kein Problem!	Das geht schon ganz gut.	Das muss ich noch üben.
Hören 👂			
Ich kann ein Gespräch über die Sehenswürdigkeiten von Kapstadt verstehen und die Informationen wiedergeben. (WB 5)	☐	☐	☐
Ich kann einem Telefonat folgen und Fragen dazu beantworten. (TB 7)	☐	☐	☐
Ich kann Vermutungen darüber anstellen, worum es in einem Song geht. (TB 13)	☐	☐	☐
Sprechen 👄			
Ich kann ausdrücken, was ich über Südafrika weiß und denke. (TB 1)	☐	☐	☐
Ich kann Fragen zu einem Text beantworten. (TB 2)	☐	☐	☐
Ich kann einem Partner/einer Partnerin Fragen stellen. (TB 4, WB 4)	☐	☐	☐
Lesen 👓			
Ich kann englische Abkürzungen in SMS verstehen. (TB 3)	☐	☐	☐
Ich kann eine Seite aus einem Reiseführer so gut verstehen, dass ich mich zu den Sehenswürdigkeiten äußern kann. (TB 5)	☐	☐	☐
Ich kann Erfahrungsberichte von Südafrikanern, die während der Apartheid gelebt haben, verstehen und ihnen Informationen entnehmen. (TB 13)	☐	☐	☐
Schreiben ✏️			
Ich kann SMS auf Englisch verfassen. (TB 3)	☐	☐	☐
Ich kann einen Zeitstrahl zu Nelson Mandelas Leben anlegen. (TB 12)	☐	☐	☐
Wortschatz 🗃️			
Ich kann Wörter zum Thema Verreisen mit dem Flugzeug erklären. (WB 3)	☐	☐	☐
LERN- UND ARBEITSTECHNIKEN 🔧			
Ich kann mir Notizen machen, um Fragen zu beantworten. (TB 2)	☐	☐	☐
Ich kann anhand von Bildern Vermutungen anstellen und diese dann mithilfe eines Hörtextes überprüfen. (TB 10, TB 11)	☐	☐	☐

	Kein Problem!	Das geht schon ganz gut.	Das muss ich noch üben.

Hören

Ich kann eine Tornado-Warnung verstehen und daraus entnehmen, wie ich mich zu verhalten habe. (TB 6)

Ich kann einem Dialog über eine Naturkatastrophe folgen. (WB 5)

Ich kann mir zu einem Radiointerview Notizen machen. (TB 13)

Sprechen

Ich kann mich mit einem Partner/einer Partnerin über den Inhalt eines Zeitungsartikels austauschen. (TB 2)

Ich kann die Unterschiede zwischen zwei Zeitungsartikeln erläutern. (TB 4)

Ich kann an einer Diskussion teilnehmen und Zustimmung oder Ablehnung ausdrücken. (TB 15)

Lesen

Ich kann einem Zeitungsartikel eine Überschrift zuordnen. (TB 4)

Ich kann Aussagen Informationen entnehmen. (TB 12)

Schreiben

Ich kann einen Bericht aus der Sicht eines Überlebenden einer Naturkatastrophe schreiben. (TB 5)

Wortschatz

Ich kann Wörtern Definitionen zuordnen. (TB 1)

Ich kann mit Vokabular aus dem Wortfeld Technologie umgehen. (TB 9, 10)

LERN- UND ARBEITSTECHNIKEN

Ich kann anhand mehrerer Beispiele eigene Definitionen erstellen. (TB 1)

Hier findest du ein paar Tipps, die dir helfen sollen, dich ideal auf deine Prüfung am Ende der 10. Klasse vorzubereiten.

WO

Du solltest dich dort, wo du lernst, wohlfühlen. Das ist wichtig, damit du die Zeit, die du mit Lernen verbringst, so gut wie möglich nutzen kannst.

* Suche dir einen ruhigen Ort und mach es dir bequem.
* Dein Lernort sollte gut ausgeleuchtet sein.
* Es sollte möglichst leise sein, damit du dich konzentrieren kannst. Mach also lieber keine laute Musik an.
* Lerne nicht in einem Raum des Hauses, in dem du leicht abgelenkt werden könntest, also z.B. nicht in der Nähe des Fernsehers.

WIE

Es gibt einige nützliche Methoden, mit deren Hilfe du dir gewisse Dinge besser merken kannst.

* Notiere dir Ideen und kurze Fakten auf Karteikarten, die du dann als Hilfen verwendest.
* Schreibe wichtige Dinge, z.B. Grammatikregeln, auf kleine Zettel und hänge diese überall im Haus auf. So siehst du sie immer wieder.
* Lerne gemeinsam mit einem Freund/einer Freundin. Ihr könnt euch gegenseitig testen.
* Versuche, alte Prüfungsaufgaben zu machen. (Oft kannst du die Prüfungen der letzten Jahre (mit Lösungen) im Internet finden.) So lernst du, auf die Zeit zu achten.
* Mach nicht stundenlang das Gleiche, sondern versuche ein bisschen Ablenkung in dein Lernen zu bringen.
* Achte darauf, die ein oder andere Pause einzulegen, regelmäßig zu trinken und zu essen und dich auch mal zu entspannen.
*

WANN

- Am einfachsten und stressfreiesten wird das Lernen, wenn du einen genauen Plan hast. So weißt du immer, was du als Nächstes tun musst.
- Mindestens sechs Wochen vor deinen Prüfungen solltest du mit dem Lernen anfangen.
- Mach dir einen Zeitplan für jede Woche. Vergiss deine regelmäßigen Verpflichtungen, z.B. deinen Nebenjob oder dein Sporttraining, nicht. Häng deinen Zeitplan dort auf, wo du ihn gut sehen kannst
- Erstell eine Liste mit allen Fächern und Themen, die du für deine Abschlussprüfungen lernen musst.
- Erkundige dich was, du für die Prüfungen wissen musst. Dann merkst du schnell, in welchen Bereichen du noch Lücken hast. Arbeite gezielt an diesen Bereichen.
- Plane mehr Zeit für die Dinge ein, die dir noch schwerfallen.
- Versuche, so oft wie möglich zu lernen. Mach lieber jeden Tag ein bisschen, als tagelang nichts zu tun und dann alles auf einmal lernen zu wollen.
- Kalkuliere Freizeit mit ein. Du solltest regelmäßige Pausen machen und auch mal frische Luft schnappen können.
- Nach einer Pause kann es gut tun, das Fach oder das Thema zu wechseln, damit dir nicht zu langweilig wird.

IN DER PRÜFUNG

Keine Panik! Denk immer positiv.

- Es ist ganz natürlich, dass du vor der Prüfung nervös bist, aber wenn du deine Vorbereitung gut planst und gewissenhaft durchführst, dann wirst du die Prüfung viel gelassener angehen können.
- Um unnötigen Stress zu vermeiden, informiere dich genau:
  wann und wo die Prüfung stattfindet
  wie lang die Prüfung sein wird wie viele Fragen du beantworten musst.
- Stell sicher, dass du alles dabei hast, was du brauchst (Stifte, Papier, Wörterbuch usw.)
  eine Uhr dabei hast, um den Überblick über die Zeit zu behalten, und pünktlich da bist.
- Wenn du in der Prüfung bist, schau dir zunächst alle Fragen an und markiere die Aufgaben, von denen du denkst, dass sie dir am schwersten fallen werden. Achte darauf, dass du dir die Zeit so einteilst, dass du alle Fragen beantworten kannst.
- Schau dir die Arbeitsanweisungen genau an, bevor du loslegst.
- Am Ende solltest du dir auf alle Fälle zehn Minuten Zeit nehmen, um dir deine Antworten noch einmal durchzulesen.

infinitive	simple past	past participle	German
draw / drɔ: /	drew / dru: /	drawn / drɔ:n /	zeichnen
dream / dri:m /	dreamt/dreamed / dremt/dri:md /	dreamt/dreamed / dremt/dri:md /	träumen
drink / drɪŋk /	drank / dræŋk /	drunk / drʌŋk /	trinken
drive / draɪv /	drove / drəʊv /	driven / ˈdrɪvn /	fahren
eat / i:t /	ate / eɪt /	eaten / ˈi:tn /	essen
fall / fɔ:l /	fell / fel /	fallen / ˈfɔ:lən /	fallen
feed / fi:d /	fed / fed /	fed / fed /	füttern; ernähren
feel / fi:l /	felt / felt /	felt / felt /	(sich) fühlen
fight / faɪt /	fought / fɔ:t /	fought / fɔ:t /	(be)kämpfen
find / faɪnd /	found / faʊnd /	found / faʊnd /	finden
fit / fɪt /	fit/fitted / fɪt/ˈfɪtɪd /	fit/fitted / fɪt/ˈfɪtɪd /	passen (zu)
flee / fli: /	fled / fled /	fled / fled /	fliehen
fly / flaɪ /	flew / flu: /	flown / fləʊn /	fliegen
forecast / ˈfɔ:kɑ:st /	forecast / ˈfɔ:kɑ:st /	forecast / ˈfɔ:kɑ:st /	vorhersagen
forget / fəˈget /	forgot / fəˈgɒt /	forgotten / fəˈgɒtn /	vergessen
get / get /	got / gɒt /	got/gotten / gɒt/ˈgɒtn /	bekommen; (an)kommen; verstehen; werden
give / gɪv /	gave / geɪv /	given / ˈgɪvn /	geben
go / gəʊ /	went / went /	gone / gɒn /	gehen; fahren
grow / grəʊ /	grew / gru: /	grown / grəʊn /	wachsen; anbauen
hang / hæŋ /	hung / hʌŋ /	hung / hʌŋ /	(auf)hängen
have / hæv /	had / hæd /	had / hæd /	haben; essen
hear / hɪə /	heard / hɜ:d /	heard / hɜ:d /	hören
hide / haɪd /	hid / hɪd /	hidden / ˈhɪdn /	(sich) verstecken
hit / hɪt /	hit / hɪt /	hit / hɪt /	schlagen; treffen; stoßen (gegen); erschüttern
hold / həʊld /	held / held /	held / held /	halten; veranstalten
keep / ki:p /	kept / kept /	kept / kept /	(be)halten; aufbewahren
know / nəʊ /	knew / nju: /	known / nəʊn /	wissen; kennen
lead / li:d /	led / led /	led / led /	(an)führen, leiten
lean / li:n /	leant/leaned / lent/li:nd /	leant/leaned / lent/li:nd /	(sich) lehnen
learn / lɜ:n /	learnt/learned / lɜ:nt/lɜ:nd /	learnt/learned / lɜ:nt/lɜ:nd /	lernen
leave / li:v /	left / left /	left / left /	verlassen; abfahren; lassen
let / let /	let / let /	let / let /	lassen
lie / laɪ /	lay / leɪ /	lain / leɪn /	liegen
light / laɪt /	lit / lɪt /	lit / lɪt /	erhellen; anzünden
lose / lu:z /	lost / lɒst /	lost / lɒst /	verlieren
make / meɪk /	made / meɪd /	made / meɪd /	machen
mean / mi:n /	meant / ment /	meant / ment /	bedeuten; meinen
meet / mi:t /	met / met /	met / met /	(sich) treffen; kennenlernen
mow / məʊ /	mowed / məʊd /	mowed/mown / məʊd/məʊn /	mähen
pay / peɪ /	paid / peɪd /	paid / peɪd /	(be)zahlen
put / pʊt /	put / pʊt /	put / pʊt /	setzen, legen, stellen

infinitive	simple past	past participle	German
read / ri:d /	read / red /	read / red /	lesen
rebuild / ˌriːˈbɪld /	rebuilt / ˌriːˈbɪlt /	rebuilt / ˌriːˈbɪlt /	wieder aufbauen
ride / raɪd /	rode / rəʊd /	ridden / ˈrɪdn /	fahren; reiten
ring / rɪŋ /	rang / ræŋ /	rung / rʌŋ /	klingeln, läuten
rise / raɪz /	rose / rəʊz /	risen / ˈrɪzn /	(auf)steigen; ansteigen
run / rʌn /	ran / ræn /	run / rʌn /	laufen, rennen; betreiben, führen
say / seɪ /	said / sed /	said / sed /	sagen
see / siː /	saw / sɔː /	seen / siːn /	sehen
sell / sel /	sold / səʊld /	sold / səʊld /	verkaufen
send / send /	sent / sent /	sent / sent /	(zu)schicken
sew / səʊ /	sewed / səʊd /	sewn / səʊn /	nähen
shake / ʃeɪk /	shook / ʃʊk /	shaken / ˈʃeɪkən /	schütteln; zittern
shine / ʃaɪn /	shone / ʃɒn /	shone / ʃɒn /	scheinen (Sonne)
show / ʃəʊ /	showed / ʃəʊd /	shown / ʃəʊn /	zeigen
sing / sɪŋ /	sang / sæŋ /	sung / sʌŋ /	singen
sit / sɪt /	sat / sæt /	sat / sæt /	sitzen
sleep / sliːp /	slept / slept /	slept / slept /	schlafen
sneak / sniːk /	snuck / snʌk /	snuck / snʌk /	schleichen
speak / spiːk /	spoke / spəʊk /	spoken / ˈspəʊkən /	sprechen, reden
spell / spel /	spelt/spelled / spelt/speld /	spelt/spelled / spelt/speld /	buchstabieren
spend / spend /	spent / spent /	spent / spent /	ausgeben (Geld); verbringen (Zeit)
spit / spɪt /	spit/spat / spɪt/spæt /	spit/spat / spɪt/spæt /	spucken
split / splɪt /	split / splɪt /	split / splɪt /	(sich) teilen; sich abspalten
spread / spred /	spread / spred /	spread / spred /	(sich) verbreiten, (sich) ausbreiten
stand / stænd /	stood / stʊd /	stood / stʊd /	stehen; ertragen, aushalten
steal / stiːl /	stole / stəʊl /	stolen / ˈstəʊlən /	stehlen, klauen
strike / straɪk /	struck / strʌk /	struck / strʌk /	(zu)schlagen; treffen
swim / swɪm /	swam / swæm /	swum / swʌm /	schwimmen
take / teɪk /	took / tʊk /	taken / ˈteɪkən /	(mit)nehmen; bringen; brauchen, dauern
teach / tiːtʃ /	taught / tɔːt /	taught / tɔːt /	unterrichten; beibringen
tell / tel /	told / təʊld /	told / təʊld /	erzählen; sagen
think / θɪŋk /	thought / θɔːt /	thought / θɔːt /	denken, glauben, meinen
throw / θrəʊ /	threw / θruː /	thrown / θrəʊn /	werfen
understand / ˌʌndəˈstænd /	understood / ˌʌndəˈstænd /	understood / ˌʌndəˈstænd /	verstehen
wear / weə /	wore / wɔː /	worn / wɔːn /	tragen (Kleidung)
win / wɪn /	won / wʌn /	won / wʌn /	gewinnen
write / raɪt /	wrote / rəʊt /	written / ˈrɪtn /	schreiben

QUELLENVERZEICHNIS

Bildquellen

Umschlagfoto: Dirk Schmidt/dsphotos.de; 123RF.com, Hong Kong: 28 (zatletic); alamy images, Abingdon/Oxfordshire: 30 (Photofusion Picture Library / Maggie Murray), 36 (Realimage), 39 (Top-Pics TBK), 94 (Richard Jupe), 95 (David Askham); dsphotos.de, Hamburg: Titel; fotolia.com, New York: 28, 30 (Phototom), 36 (grafikplusfoto), 39 (Fotowahn), 39 (biamiti), 39 (tarei), 39 (Andrea Vonblon), 46 (UTOPIA), 46 (Shumba138), 55 (Michael Jung); Getty Images, München: 8 (Michael Ochs Archives), 30 (Taxi / Dennis Felix), 48 (2009 / Chris Jackson); images.com, New York: 14 (Jose Giribas); Interfoto, München: 5 (Miller), 5 (Miller), 5 (Argam), 5 (Miller), 5 (Miller), 5 (Argam); iStockphoto.com, Calgary: 14 (sturti), 28 (Katarzyna Bialasiewicz), 30 (paresh3d), 30 (zorani), 30 (Likhitha), 55; Keystone Schweiz, Frankfurt/M.: 14 (Jochen Zick); Picture-Alliance GmbH, Frankfurt/M.: 14 (Angelika Warmuth), 14 (reality), 23 (dpa), 23 (dpa), 30 (Carsten Schmidt), 30 (Ulrich Malisius), 94 (Image Source), 98 (Christoph Hardt/Geisler-Fotopress), 98 (gbrci/Geisler-Fotopress); Shutterstock.com, New York: 13 (Jorg Hackemann), 28 (StanislavBeloglazov), 36 (AlenD), 57 (Akhenaton Images), 59 (koya979), 59 (Igor Klimov), 59 (bmaki), 59 (Nikuwka), 59 (photostock77), 73 (lassedesignen), 94 (oleksa); terre des hommes Deutschland e.V., Osnabrück: 23.

Textquellen

40   https://simple.wikipedia.org/wiki/Apartheid

THEME 1

2 Seite 3

Lösungsbeispiel: Joan Lingard is the author of the book 'Across the barricades'. She is a British writer and she was born in Edinburgh in 1932. She grew up in Belfast and lived there until she was 18 years old. She started to write when she was only eleven years old. In 1970, she published her first children's book called 'The Twelfth Day of July'. It was part of a series of books, and 'Across the barricades' is the second book in the series. The book is about Kevin, who is a Catholic, and Sadie, who is a Protestant, who live in Northern Ireland. They fall in love and they are caught up in the troubles in Northern Ireland.

3 Seite 4

b) Lösungsbeispiel: 1. Upset, helpless; 2. Helpless, disappointed; 3. Upset, helpless

4 Seite 4

a) Lösungsbeispiel: Paula says she really enjoyed this book although it is old. She thinks it was very interesting and moving, and she really felt for Kevin and Sadie. She thinks it's really sad and stupid that people fight over religion, and says it is hard to imagine that things were so difficult only 40 years ago. She wants to read the three books in the series after this one because she wants to know what happens next.

6 Seite 5

a) Lösungsbeispiel: In the middle picture on the left hand side, I can see a man with a gun, probably a soldier, and a man who has his hands on his head. It looks like a terrible situation. Perhaps the man was fighting against the soldier and now he feels scared about what will happen to him. It looks like they are running in the street, which is shocking for me. I would be really frightened if I saw someone with a gun in the street!

In the bottom picture on the right hand side, I can see a man who looks like he is religious. He is wearing long white clothes. There are two soldiers next to him, and they are talking to each other. I think this must show how religion and violence were connected during the Troubles in Northern Ireland. It's interesting to see how the religious man speaks to the soldiers and seems to be very calm.

b) Lösungsbeispiel: 1. The conflict was mainly about the constitutional status of Northern Ireland, and whether it should leave or stay in the United Kingdom. 2. The conflict lasted for a thirty-year period - it began in the late 1960s and lasted until 1998. 3. The conflict ended with the Good Friday Agreement of 1998.

9 Seite 7

Lösungsbeispiel: Dear Mum and Dad,
I'm sorry that this letter has to be my goodbye, but I knew that if I told you I was leaving, you would try to stop me. I know you only want the best for me,

but I'm sick of the bombs and the fights and all the problems here in Belfast. I can't live like this anymore, I have to be free. Kevin is going to England and I'm going with him. I know you don't understand that we love each other and that I don't care if he's a Catholic, but maybe one day you will. I hope so. Please don't worry about me.
Love,
Sadie

E2 Seite 13

Lösungsbeispiel: Kevin McCoy is 18 years old and lives in Belfast in Northern Ireland. He has eight brothers and sisters, and is Catholic. He's also an unskilled worker. He has a girlfriend called Sadie, and wants to move to London.

E4 Seite 14

Lösungsbeispiel: Travel – gap year, with friends, save money from part-time job, go to every continent
Work abroad – volunteer with the IVS (International Voluntary Service), work on environmental projects
Study – decide after gap year, apply to universities in the USA and Canada, study economics or history

M4 Seite 16-17

c) Lösungsbeispiel: In the text, Manjit imagines what Lisa's relationship with her family must be like. He thinks she won't understand how much he will hurt his family if he doesn't have an arranged marriage because she is 'never going to have to choose between what she want(s) out of life and her family' (lines 26-28). He also thinks that she will never have to 'fight to be an individual' (line 29). Lisa tells Manjit that it will be fine after a while, which makes it sound like that this is what normally happens with her parents.

d) Lösungsbeispiel: When Manjit says he has to 'fight to be seen as an individual', I think he means that his family doesn't want to accept that he has his own hopes and dreams which he wants to achieve on his own. These might be different from the plans his family have for him: for example, they want him to have an arranged marriage and we know that he doesn't want this. If his family saw him as an individual, they would see that he has different opinions to them and support him anyway.

M5 Seite 17

a) Lösungsbeispiel: The summary is different to my ending of the story because I thought that Lisa and Manjit would still be a couple. I thought that Manjit's parents would give up eventually because his brothers also didn't have arranged marriages.

b) Lösungsbeispiel: I find it shocking that Manjit's parents react in such a very extreme way and decide to behave as if he doesn't exist. I thought they seemed very interested in his life and it's hard to believe that parents could ignore their own children. I also don't think they should be surprised or upset that Manjit escaped on his wedding day because he had told them many times before that this wasn't what he wanted, and they forced him to go to India.

c) Lösungsbeispiel: Do you feel that you made the right decision escaping your wedding? Do you still feel angry with your parents for what they did to you? Would you like to talk to them now? What do you want to do after you take your GCSEs? Have you told Jenny about what happened to you?

M6 Seite 18

c) 1. I do think both parents need to look after the children. 2. You do have to keep working to be a good example. 3. I do like being at home with the kids.

M7 Seite 18

a) Lösungsbeispiel: Nick Hornby is an English writer who was born in Surrey in 1957. He went to Cambridge University and studied English there. Nick published his first book in 1992, and since then has sold more than 5 million copies of his books all over the world. His most famous books are Fever Pitch, High Fidelity and About a Boy. Several of his books have been made into successful films. His books are often about music and sport. Nick also writes lyrics for music artists and film scripts.

b) Lösungsbeispiel: SLAM was published in the United Kingdom in 2007. The main theme of the book is teenage pregnancy, and the main character is a 16-year-old teenage named Sam, who lives in London and likes skateboarding. Sam has a girlfriend called Alicia, who gets pregnant and doesn't want to have an abortion. The book is about how Sam and Alicia deal with the situation and with being teenage parents. SLAM is Nick Hornby's first book for young adults, and he decided to write it because he noticed more and more teenagers were coming to hear him read his books. The book was generally successful and received good reviews.

THEME 2

1 Seite 19

b) Lösungsbeispiel: I really do have a lot of plans for the future. First, I want to live in another country and enjoy being independent. I want to learn new languages and make lots of international friends. Then, I want to live in a city in England and focus on my career. I would like to be active and outgoing, and see my friends regularly. I would also like to have children, but not until after I have travelled to all five continents and had adventures with my friends or with my partner. I want to buy my own house or flat, and have dogs and cats. Eventually I would probably like to get married, but I know it can be very expensive. What I know I wouldn't want to do is be famous, or have a boring job, even if I earned a lot of money from it.

6 Seite 22

b) Lösungsbeispiel: I am able to apply for jobs in English. I can talk to foreign guests. My English is good enough to look for information on English websites. I can read children's books in English. I am able to understand radio programmes.

9 Seite 24

c) Lösungsbeispiel: Picture A looks like child labour. The boy is working on a factory machine that produces cotton. A child wouldn't do this kind of physical work at home. Picture B looks like a chore. The girl is emptying the dishwasher and tidying up. She is in a kitchen and this is a normal job that young people have to do at home. Picture C looks like child labour. The picture is in black and white and is very old, and you can see two boys with bare feet standing on a machine and working. It must be child labour because it looks very dangerous and it would probably be illegal today. Picture D looks like a chore. It shows a boy mowing the lawn. It looks like hard work, but he seems to be doing it in a garden, so he is probably at home and doesn't have to do this all day to earn money. Picture E looks like child labour. A little boy is making bricks outside, and he isn't wearing any shoes. He doesn't look old enough or prepared for this job, and this is not a normal job parents give to their children at home. Picture F looks like a chore. A girl is hoovering the floor, and there are other people in the background. These could be family members. She is wearing comfortable clothes and it looks like she is at home, so this is probably not child labour.

E5 Seite 30

Lösungsbeispiel: I think it's good that children do chores at home. It helps them to learn skills for the future, because nobody can avoid chores when they are an adult! However, I think it's a bit silly when really young children do chores like vacuuming or cleaning, because they can't do it properly and they don't understand that it's a responsibility. Of course, it's important that both boys and girls learn household skills. If your parents work all day, it's only fair that children help to keep the house clean and cook food for when they come home.

M1 Seite 31

a) Lösungsbeispiel: Dear students,

we are really interested in how you choose your future job in England, and what the different options are after you've left school. We will soon have to make decisions about our futures, too. We would like to know if any of you have plans yet, and what these plans are - and if you don't know yet, how are you going to find out what you want to do?

Bye for now,

Class 10

b) Lösungsbeispiel: Ben has been writing applications for three months. Aaron has collected model aeroplanes since he was little.
Melinda has been helping her grandfather to check the car for a long time.
Kate has wanted to become a hairdresser since she was five years old.

c) Lösungsbeispiel: Hi Melinda,
From your email, it sounds like you really do enjoy working with cars. You've already done a month of work experience, so why not go for it and start looking for an apprenticeship? What your mum says isn't true – parents can be so old and boring sometimes. Things are different now, and she probably just wants you to be happy. If you explain to her that this is something you're really interested in, I'm sure she'll accept it after a while. I know this sounds difficult, but you don't want to get a job you don't like!
Best wishes, Helen

M4   Seite 32
b) 2. He set up Amdale with his ex-wife. 4. Martin's company employs 22 people. 5. Martin's company produces brake pedals for Formula 1 cars.

M5   Seite 33
c) Lösungsbeispiel: Dear Mr McHoggart,
I have seen your advertisement for a certified welder and am very interested in the position. Please find attached my CV, which contains details on my employment history, qualifications and skills.
I have been working as a qualified welder for RSH GmbH in Neustadt since 2014, which means that I am very experienced with the job and have all the necessary qualifications. During this time I have also travelled around southern Germany to work on various projects with various teams, which means that I am a very flexible worker and consider myself as a team player. Having studied English and Spanish at school and being a German native speaker, I am also well-prepared to work internationally.
Please contact me if you would like any other information, and I look forward to hearing from you.
Yours sincerely,
Kevin Hofer

THEME 3

1   Seite 36
Lösungsbeispiel: Mia is bad at playing football. Norman is fond of chatting. Johan loves travelling.

5   Seite 38
b) Lösungsbeispiel: Table Mountain: most prominent landmark, amazing, great, see Cape Town from above, get a feeling of the layout before you explore the town ; Khayelitsha Township: second largest in South Africa, white government forced black people to live there during apartheid, black people not allowed to live in city centres, now still mostly poor

black people live there, government trying to improve living conditions; V&A Waterfront: one of Baruti's favourite places, can sit, have a coffee, watch people, brilliant view of the bay; Boo Kap: district where lots of Muslims live, ancestors brought here as slaves from Malay, colourful houses, Malayan food very good

6   Seite 38
a) Lösungsbeispiel: Isabel says that her visit to Robben Island was very interesting. The stories told by the guide about how hard life was in the prison made her feel terribly sad. She said that she almost cried because it was so moving and emotional.

E2   Seite 44
Lösungsbeispiel: Nelson Rolihlahla Mandela was born on July 18th 1918 and died on December 5th 2013. He married three times in his life, and had six children. He is famous because he was an anti-apartheid revolutionary and a political leader. He was President of South Africa from 1994 to 1999. He spent 27 years in prison for his fight against apartheid. In 1993, he received the Nobel Peace Prize.

M4   Seite 48
b) Lösungsbeispiel: Nelson Mandela was the leader of the government which oversaw the dismantling of Apartheid. He became the first black president of South Africa in 1994 and championed social justice until his death in 2013. Before this, he had been viewed as a terrorist by world media as the leader of the ANC and had spent a total of 27 years in prison. The Nelson Mandela 70th Birthday Tribute, held in 1988 at Wembley Stadium, aimed to raise worldwide awareness of his imprisonment and succeeded.

THEME 4

1   Seite 50
Lösungsbeispiel: Trees can be uprooted. Emergency shelters should be set up. Areas are searched.

3   Seite 51
Lösungsbeispiel: I like the style of article 1 best as it is more exciting and really keeps your attention.
I prefer article 2 because there are more facts and the details of who, what, when and where are clearer.

4   Seite 51
a) Lösungsbeispiel: 1. My name is Mrs Jane Denton, I'm 39 years old, and I work as a surgeon in the local hospital. 2. When the tornado hit, I was luckily at home with my husband and my dog. 3. I heard the warning on the radio and immediately went down into the basement. 4. I did know what to do as tornadoes happen quite often where we live, but none has ever come so close to our town before. 5. I told my husband, and we both took the dog downstairs into the basement. We hid under a table and waited for hours and hours until the sound of the tornado had stopped. 6. I felt terrified. I knew I was doing the right thing, but it still didn't mean that we

would be safe and survive.

Dear Sir/Madam,

My name is Mrs Jane Denton. I'm 39 years old and I work as a surgeon in the local hospital in Lone Grove, which is also where I live. I was at home when the tornado hit, which I'm very glad about because it meant I was together with my husband and my dog. We were warned about the tornado on the radio. We knew that we had to get to safety, because this has happened before, although it was never as serious as this time. We went down into the basement with the dog and waited for hours until we thought it must be safe to come out. We hid under a table down there and we could hear the tornado damaging our house above us. I thought the roof might be gone when we came out, but I didn't expect the whole house to have gone. But it was. It was a terrifying experience.

Yours, Mrs Jane Denton

9 Seite 54

c) Lösungsbeispiel: I don't think it's okay to post pictures of people without asking for their permission first, even if you think the picture is really funny or nice. You should understand that not everybody feels the same about pictures of them being put online – just because you're okay with it doesn't mean that your friends are. I don't think you're a very good friend if you don't appreciate this.

E2 Seite 58

Lösungsbeispiel: Steve was at home when he heard on the radio that there was going to be a tornado. The first thing he did was go to the supermarket and buy lots of food supplies. Then he went into his basement and waited until the tornado had stopped. Afterwards, he helped clean up.

E4 Seite 59

Lösungsbeispiel: I would use the smart watch to plan a route when I go running and to check the weather before I go out. I would use the computer to play video games and do online shopping. I would use the smartphone to call and message my friends and use social networks when I am out. I would use the house phone to call company numbers and to call my grandma. I would use the typewriter to write a ghost story.

M3 Seite 62

b) Lösungsbeispiel: The person who wrote the diary entry was right about the telephones. We all have mobile phones now that we carry around all the time. They were also right about telephone calls – it's very easy now to call people in different countries, and often really cheap! The person was wrong about letters though – it's sad, but almost nobody writes letters to their friends or family anymore because they can send emails instead. That way, we don't have to wait long for replies. I really like their idea about waterproof paper, but perhaps we haven't invented that yet because we can write everything on

computers and save it online now instead.

M4 Seite 62

b) Lösungsbeispiel: Advantages: can contact people and make friends without going anywhere, don't have to talk to anybody, see what's happening in everyone's lives, keep in touch with friends you meet on holiday or who live somewhere else now, chat with friends whenever you want, play online games, watch videos on all kinds of topics

Disadvantages: could do better things with your time, should go out more often and meet friends, you don't see the other person's face, sometimes people post stupid things they wouldn't say in person, using your mobile too much can cause headaches and sleeplessness, hard to turn your mobile off as you feel like you're missing out on important things, can encounter pornography or violence

I agree that online communication is great for keeping in touch with friends you don't see regularly anymore. It used to be very expensive to make phone calls abroad, and on social networks, you can message and video call to the same places for free! I also agree that it's nice to be able to see what your friends are doing when you're not with them, but I think worrying that you'll miss important things when you go offline is just silly. Nothing people post online can be that important. However useful online communication can be, it's definitely true that we all go out and meet our friends in person less than we used to, and that's not very healthy.

c) Lösungsbeispiel: "It's obvious that you shouldn't believe everything that is written and said online." It should be obvious that not everything on the Internet is true, but it's easy to forget. When you search for information online about a particular topic, you often click on and read the first website you find and presume that it's going to give you facts, when it could have been written by someone unreliable or someone who wants to support a particular opinion. Old people especially, who haven't got as much experience with the Internet as young people, are more likely to believe everything they read online. I mostly agree with the statement.

"I feel free without my smartphone."
I definitely feel free without my smartphone. Whenever I do something that doesn't involve my smartphone, like drawing or playing sports, I feel proud of myself. I like to have it nearby so that I can check for messages if I need to, but it feels good to not play on it all the time. I also like to read on the bus when everyone else is playing on their phones. I know this isn't the same as turning my smartphone off, or putting it away, because I never do that, but it's better than staring at it for hours every day!

"I could probably do better things with my time than be online."
I try to only go online to reply to messages my friends

have sent me, or to send messages to friends I haven't spoken to in a long time. That way, I don't spend hours and hours exploring the internet, because it's so easy to watch one video and then immediately move on to another one! I don't think I go online too much, but I still think I could go online less and use my time better.

THEME 5

W4 Seite 74

Lösungsbeispiel:

Dear Rachel,

I know exactly how you feel. I had a problem like that a few months ago. I went out with this great guy but my parents had heard all kinds of stories about him and hated him althought they didn't even know him. And I was so afraid all the time that someone would see us and tell my parents.

After about four weeks I couldn't stand the situation any more so I just told my parents about John. And I told them that they were silly because they didn't like someone they had never met. My parents looked at each other and started laughing and told me I was right and I should ask John to come over so they could meet him and now they get along fine.

So I think you shouldn't be afraid of your parents and tell them what you think. They should at least give you a chance.

I hope everything works out.

Lots of love, Yasemin

W6 Seite 76

Lösungsbeispiele:

2. The perfect wedding

If and when I get married, I would like to have a very special wedding. I would love to get married on a tropical beach. My future husband and I would wear white clothes – but no shoes. I would invite both of our families and all of our friends. We would have a ceremony at the beach and afterwards a lovely dinner in beach huts. Maybe we could all go swimming. After dinner there would be a band and a lot of dancing. At midnight I would like to have fireworks and a really big cake. After the party we would spend our honeymoon travelling. I would love to visit New York and London and spend some more time on a tropical island.

3. Potsdam – a town to enjoy

The historical buildings and parks make Potsdam one of the most beautiful towns in Germany. If you are in Berlin, it's easy to go on a day trip to Potsdam and you should not miss out on Sanssouci, the castle built by Frederick the Great, and the old part of town. If you are interested in films, you should plan a tour of Babelsberg, the UFA film studios, where a lot of famous films have been made.

If you want to stay longer, you can choose where to spend your night: from campsites to luxurious hotels, there is a bed for everyone. And the same goes for food: Potsdam has a wide variety of restaurants, bistros and cafés.

4. Dear diary,

I just got back from our end-of-year trip to Rome. IT WAS BRILLIANT!! The whole class chose, organised and went on the trip. Even our teacher Mr XXXXX was lots of fun! We went by bus, which took 12 hours. We drove through the night so we could sleep on the bus. But we didn't sleep that much! Tim had brought lots of sweets and soft drinks with him, and we were far too excited to sleep. That didn't stop us enjoying ourselves, though. We saw Vatican City, the Spanish Steps, the Trevi fountain and the Colosseum. The highlight was the food, though … all that pizza! And pasta! And ice cream! Yummy.

We stayed in a youth hostel for one night, where I shared a room with three of my friends. The next night we had to drive back to school.

I will never forget this trip. The funniest moment was when Jan tried to secretly go into the girls' room in the hostel but got caught by Mrs XXXXX.

5. What a day!

My family and I are in London for the weekend. We are having an amazing time, but today something crazy happened.

We went to Buckingham Palace to see the guards and the buildings. It was cool to see but a little bit boring, as nothing happened. Then we went for lunch in an Italian restaurant in the area. We were starving so we all ordered huge pizzas. Delicious! Then the door opened and a huge group of people walked in and the staff at the restaurant were suddenly very stressed. It was Eminem, my favourite rapper! I just had to get an autograph …

I found a napkin on the table and a pen in my bag and took a few deep breaths before I went over to his table.

"Uh … Hi … Eminem … I'm your BIGGEST fan … I mean … sorry … I know you have lots of fans … but … I LOVE your work …" I was so nervous I was not able to finish my sentences properly!

"Hi … Nice to meet you. What's your name?"

"My name is Hannes."

"Well, Hannes … that sounds like a German name. Are you from Germany?"

"Yes, I am. My family is here for the weekend."

"Have you ever been to England before?"

"No. Never. It's my first time."

"You speak very good English for someone that has never been to England before!"

"I learn it at school. And I listen to your music a lot. It's very difficult to understand sometimes but I practise and can rap some of your songs."

"Wow, Hannes … I'd love to see that. I'm going to be performing in London tonight. How about you come to my show and I'll get you on stage to help me for a song. Would you like that?"

"Are you serious?! That would be incredible! … Can my brother come, too?"

"Sure. Bring the whole family!"

"Wow. Thank you so much."

… And it did happen! I got to rap my favourite song on stage with my favourite rapper in London … Wait till I tell people at school!

It was definitely the best day of my life. The only problem … I forgot to get his autograph!

6. James was walking home after school. He was in a terrible mood. The coolest girl in the class had asked his best friend on a date, and Tom had agreed! Tom KNEW that James liked Annabel, too. Surely he should have said no.

Suddenly, James saw a pink phone on the ground. He picked it up quickly and looked around. There was nobody in the street. What should he do?

Before he could think about it anymore, Beyoncé's newest song started playing from the phone. It was ringing! Should he answer it?

"Hello?" he answered.

"Hello!? Who are you?", came a girl's voice. "That's my phone! I must have dropped it. I need it back!"

James immediately said, "Of course. I'm in town. I can meet you at the main entrance to the park to give it back to you in ten minutes."

"Oh thank god!", said the voice.

"But how will I know it's you?", asked James.

"I'm wearing a top with roses on, black jeans, and I'm carrying a green bag", said the girl.

"And your name …?", said James, but she was gone …

James walked to the park. He was excited about meeting the owner of the phone, but it still didn't make him feel better about what his friend Tom had done.

James got to the park and immediately saw a girl standing at the entrance. Wow, she is beautiful!, he thought.

"Hello?", he said to the girl, whose name he still didn't know.

"Hello! Do you have my phone?!", she asked immediately.

"Yes, I do", said James as he gave it to her.

"Thank you so so much! You are the kindest stranger." The girl smiled. "How can I show you how grateful I am?"

"Well, …", said James. "How about a date?"

"OK!", came the reply.

"But first, your name?"

"Julie."

"Nice to meet you, Julie. I'm James. Now, when can I take you on a date?"

"How about now?"

"Wow, OK!"

Amazing, thought James, as he was walking into a café with his beautiful date. Just wait till Tom hears about this!

W7 Seite 77

Lösungsbeispiele:

2. Most people in the world today have a mobile phone and access to a computer. Would we survive if somebody took all the computers and mobile phones away? Over twenty years ago this is what the world was like. Now that we are used to these gadgets, many people think that we wouldn't be able to live without them.

I think it would be harder to live without mobile phones. Let me give you an example: If your train is late, it is very easy to let other people know that you won't be on time. Before we had mobile phones, this was not possible.

However, in my opinion, you can survive without a computer because you can find a lot of the information that is on the Internet in local libraries, newspapers or on the television or radio. Instead of typing, you can just write by hand using a pen and paper – people did it for years before computers were invented. *(162 words)*

3. Some people say that teenagers' lives are much easier today, but I'm not so sure. If you don't have the latest mobile phone or MP3 player, you could be picked on by other teenagers. Bullies now use the Internet and text messages, too, to bully their victims. On the one hand, it is easier in some ways for teenagers to be more independent from their parents because they have their own mobile phones and their own computers. But that doesn't always mean they have more privacy because news travels fast with all the new technology.

Teenagers have always had problems in life because it is a time when you go from being a child to being an adult and you are often misunderstood.

So, all in all, I think life for teenagers today is harder than it was thirty years ago. *(141 words)*

4. After finishing school, many teenagers either find a job or go travelling. What if they had to do a compulsory volunteer or social year instead? Many people think that this is a good idea, but I disagree.

Firstly, I'd like to say that I support volunteer work. There are many great organizations, such as UNICEF, that can't afford to pay all the people that work for them.

I also think you can learn a lot of new skills when doing volunteer work. For example, a lot of teenagers who go travelling do volunteer work in another country. Through this, they learn how to build schools etc. If it was compulsory, however, they might not enjoy it.

Some people also need to work so that they can earn money. Volunteer work is unpaid so they would have to depend on money from their parents or the government.

For these reasons I think that volunteer work should be optional. *(157 words)*

5. It's a fact that when young people finish school they often have two choices: to start working or find something else to do. Instead of working, many decide to travel.

I believe this is a good idea because they can visit different countries and experience different cultures. Teenagers deserve a break after working hard at school, and I believe that travelling without your parents is a good way to learn how to be independent.

Some people say that school leavers are too young to travel and that it is too expensive, but I disagree. Here is an example: You can earn money while you are travelling by working on farms or in cafés. You could also learn new skills, such as a new language, which may even help you get a better job when you return. That's why I think that if you do not have a job, you should go travelling. *(152 words)*

6. More and more women are waiting until they are older before they have children. They do this so that they can continue working for longer and earn more money and maybe get a better job. Scientists say that the younger you are, the better it is for your children. Your child is less likely to be born with health problems and if you are fit, you can interact better with your children. I believe that parent-child relationships are very important and these are often made stronger by playing a sport or doing an activity together.

On the other hand, if you have children later, you will probably have more money. This means that you will be able to pay for extra music or sport classes for your child.

All in all, I don't think it matters when you have your children as long as you accept the responsibility to have and raise a child. *(154 words)*

MD1   Seite 78

Lösungsbeispiel: (Let's Sing)

Hi Annie,

What a nice idea for a present! I know which game you should get – Let's Sing! It's perfect for your dad because you said that he's into music, and the game helps you to improve your singing skills and train your voice. Your dad can also play the game with your family, too! You can play in "battle mode" and have a competition to see who is the best singer in your family.

If your dad or family likes hits from the charts, that's even better, because Let's Sing has over thirty international hits you can sing along to!

Hope that helps you to decide!

Catherine

THEME 6

R4   Seite 92

b) 1. 1 in every 15 children in Haiti live in "restavek".

2. Families send their children into "restavek" in the hope that they can lead a better life and go to school.

3. Typical chores for "restavek" children include carrying heavy buckets of water and working in the fields.

4. The "restavek" system usually ends for a child at the age of 15 because children beyond the age of 15 must be paid, or it is against the law.

W2   Seite 94

Lösungsbeispiel: (Picture B)

Spring is finally here! To celebrate, I went to the beach with some friends.

As you can see, we all went surfing. That's Florian on the left next to our surfboards and Ben is next to his car. I'm wearing my red jumper and sitting with the rest of the gang.

It was sunny, but it isn't summer yet. We were glad we had warm clothes with us on the beach. When we went surfing the water was ice cold!! It was still a lot of fun. I hope the weather is good next weekend as well!

Lösungsbeispiel: (Picture C)

What a weekend!

So, it was my friend Paul's birthday on Saturday and he got a new mountain bike from his parents. For his birthday we went cycling in the Harz Mountains. It's a really great place to visit and we spent the whole day on our bikes.

There are some great views from the top of the mountains. Luckily the mountains aren't too high, so we didn't get too tired cycling to the top!

I think Paul's favourite part of the trip was when he did some stunt jumping on his new bike – he's really good at it. That's him in the photo!

It's my birthday next month … Maybe we'll visit the Harz again. I'd love to go hiking there, too.

W3   Seite 95

Lösungsbeispiel: (Durrell Wildlife Park)

Dear Ms Boons,

I am writing to apply to work at Jersey Zoo.

I love animals and I hope to become a vet's assistant in the future. My family has always called me animal-mad and at home I look after our two dogs, three cats and four rabbits. It would be great to work with more unusual animals and to work outdoors. I have also never been to Jersey so it would be interesting to explore a new place.

I work very hard and I enjoy working in a team.

I look forward to hearing from you soon.

Yours sincerely,

Lena Böll

MD1 Seite 97

Vor dem Urlaub solltest du dich beim Arzt über nötige Impfungen und Medikamente erkundigen.

Du solltest versuchen, Insektenstichen vorzubeugen, z. B. durch Insektensprays und langärmelige Kleidung.

Am besten fasst du keine Tiere an.

Trink nur Wasser aus Flaschen.

Du solltest keine rohen oder halbrohen Lebensmittel essen.

MD2 Seite 97

1. A girl, Sophie, is looking for somebody to help her practise her English once a week. She mainly needs help with talking to others, so a native speaker would be great. She can't pay for the lessons, but is offering guitar lessons in return.

2. Tommy is worried about his friend, who spends up to ten hours on his smartphone every day. Tommy is looking for people with a similar problem, so that they can try and deal with it together.

3. Frau Albrecht is looking for a young person (16 or older) to help in a flower shop on Saturdays. They'll earn nine euros per hour. People who want to apply for the job can call her in the evening.

MD3 Seite 98

Lösungsbeispiel: (Dner)

Dner is one of the most successful and popular German Internet stars.

His real name is Felix and he was born in 1994.

He studied media at university in Cologne. He concentrates on the games Minecraft and Grand Theft Auto V. He also publishes clips from his life, such as when he did a longboard tour through Germany.

His success shows that many young YouTube stars are in demand by companies who can use them for advertising.